Generis

PUBLISHING

Faces of Corporate Liquidity Sustainability Necessary and Sufficient Conditions

José Antonio de França
Wilfredo Sosa Sandoval

Title: Faces of Corporate Liquidity Sustainability Necessary and Sufficient Conditions

ISBN: 979-8-88676-496-3

Author: José Antonio de França, Wilfredo Sosa Sandoval

Cover image: www.pixabay.com

Publisher: Generis Publishing
Online orders: www.generis-publishing.com
Contact email: info@generis-publishing.com

Content

6

Acknowledgments

This book is the result of research developed and tested in the classroom, with students from the Accounting and Actuarial Sciences course at the University of Brasília (UnB), in the Liquidity Analysis content, in several academic semesters.

Subsequently, this content was also tested in research in the postgraduate course, *stricto sensu*, in business economics, at the Catholic University of Brasília (UCB), from which I am a graduate, with the help of Professor Wilfredo Sosa Sandoval, who later developed and incorporated, to the theme, the theorem of the financially efficient firm and all algebraic conformity, now as a co-author.

So, it's these former students, graduates, now professional colleagues, and Prof. Dr. Wilfredo Sosa Sandoval, my supervisor in the PhD in economics, to whom I initially wish to express my gratitude for the partnership and companionship.

But in the development of the research I deprived myself of several moments with my family that understood my absences and allowed that literature has this humble contribution. I thank my wife and children who were able to appreciate the importance of the contribution of this work, as an addition to the existing knowledge.

Last but not least, I would like to thank Professor Paulo Roberto Barbosa Lustosa, from the Department of Accounting and Actuarial Sciences (DCCA) at the University of Brasília (UnB), my supervisor in the PhD in accounting, for the review and preface with absolute professionalism.

Professor José Antonio de França
Professor Wilfredo Sosa Sandoval

Foreword

I was very happy and honored by the invitation to preface this book. The experience of having supervised the doctoral thesis in Accounting Sciences of one of the authors, Professor José Antonio de França, and of having followed his trajectory in a second doctorate, in Economics, in a way, would allow anticipating the approach that was given in the present book. For many years, Professor França carried out the practical activities of accountant with competence. If, on the one hand, this gave him a lot of sense to deal with the concrete world, on the other hand, it may have restricted the opening of his imagination to abstract things, more connected to the cognitive abilities of relating ideas and apparently disjoint concepts.

In his late doctorate in accounting sciences, I introduced Professor França to the topic of operational leverage, with two related research questions to investigate. The first consisted of analytically identifying the deleveraging point at which the firm would be operating at the optimal level of its installed capacity. The accounting assumption of linearity of costs and revenues, valid only in the relevant production interval, leads to the false conclusion that the firm would be unleveraged when its degree of operating leverage (DOL) was equal to 1, because at that point the operating profit would not be multiplied more than proportionally to the change in revenue. But this is a logical impossibility, because for DOL to be equal to 1 the profit would have to be infinite, at the minimum point of the exponentially decreasing function DOL = f(operating profit). Then, through a graphical analysis of this function, we conclude that, in accounting terms, the firm's maximum efficiency point occurs when the DOL is equal to 2.

The second research question, derived from the first, was to empirically test whether firms with a DOL in the neighborhood of 2, with revenue variation control, had relatively higher economic performance, as measured by the market, than leveraged firms with a DOL increasingly greater than 2. The results confirmed the theoretical expectation. But much more important than the results of this thesis was the enchantment of the knowledge that this experience generated in Professor França. He realized the challenges he had to face to overcome his limitations if he wanted to delve deep into the world of quantitative methodology research in applied social sciences, which was the case. He understood the importance of intensive reading of research published in the best international journals in the area, knowledge of the great supporting theories, a reasonable mastery of instrumental disciplines, such as mathematics and statistics, and scripts and technological tools for data analysis.

Dazzled by the new world that was unfolding in front of him, which until then was unknown to him, Professor França accepted the challenge of facing it and decided to do a second doctorate, now in Economics, where he was supervised by the co-author of this book, the mathematician Professor Doctor Wilfredo Sosa Sandoval. The new enchantment now, I venture to conjecture, is about the perhaps limitless possibilities of connecting two languages, accounting and mathematics, for the exploration and investigation of organizational problems. And here I return to my initial statement, that a careful observation of Professor França's trajectory during his two doctorates allows us to understand the focus given to the content of this book.

The book consists of four chapters, all related to the current liquidity topic of organizations. The approach brings innovative contributions in relation to the static concept of liquidity, commonly described in textbooks on financial management, by exploring the relationship of this variable with other constructs extracted from financial statements. Clearly, the authors' interest in connecting the accounting language, as an information and communication system, with the mathematical language can be clearly seen. It is also evident the use of abstract reasoning in the definition of liquidity and solvency accounting constructs, as well as in their relationship with other accounting concepts not directly observable.

The second chapter abstracts from vertical, horizontal and diagonal movements between the aggregate current and non-current balance sheet components, and vice versa, to derive incremental and dynamic information content from the current liquidity ratio. The dynamics of the migration of these aggregates, between different fiscal years, shows that the current liquidity index varies randomly and non-linearly over time, which makes it difficult to definitively conclude on the firm's liquidity based only on its static short-term liquidity position. deadline.

The third chapter brings a bolder conceptual flight. It defines the variable operating performance versus financial solvency (OPFS) as a direct function of the degree of operating leverage (DOL) and an inverse function of the current liquidity ratio (CR). Comparing these two dimensionless measures, three levels of OPFS are established ($1 \leq OPFS < 1$), based on the comparison of the DOL with the CR, it is concluded that the lower the OPFS, in relation to the CR, the more efficient the firm is in the generation of net current assets with the capacity to support short-term debt.

In the fourth chapter, the current liquidity index is related to the measures of the level of activity that characterize the operational and financial cycles of the firm, commonly derived in the literature from the average terms of receipt of sales, renewal or retention of inventories, and payment for purchases. Based on these relationships, the financial efficiency coefficient (CEF) and the liquidity sustainability coefficient (LSR) are defined, based on which the firm is classified, in terms of liquidity, as strongly sustainable, weakly sustainable, or not sustainable.

The four chapters were written in the format of academic articles. At the same time, there are typical textbook elements, such as tables with liquidity formulas and learning assessment quizzes at the end of each chapter. Perhaps it is necessary to analyze the most appropriate way of marketing this work, depending on its objectives. In any case, I leave here my satisfaction and joy for realizing the evident progress of my friend, Professor França, in the difficult, continuous and pleasant path of the expansion of consciousness through science.

Professor Paulo Roberto B. Lustosa
University of Brasilia

List of Acronyms

π	Profit
ALP	Analysis of Liquidity Properties
AT	Acid Test Ratio
CA	Current Assets
CGS	Cost of Goods Sold
CL	Current Liabilities
CM	Contribution margin
CR	Current Ratio
DOL	Degree of Operating Leverage
DPO	Days Payable Outstanding
DSI	Days Sales of Inventory
DSO	Days Sales Outstanding
FA	Fixed Assets
FC	Financial Cycle
FE	Fixed costs and expenses
FER	Financial Efficiency Ratio
GP	Gross Purchases
GR	General Ratio
LSR	Liquidity Sustainability Ratio
LTL	Long-term Liabilities
LTNC	Long-term net capital
NCA	Non-Current Assets
NCL	Non-Current Liabilities
NE	Net Equity
NI	Neutral Interactions
NR	Net Revenue
NSC	Necessary and Sufficient Condition
NWC	Net Working Capital
OC	Operating Cycle
OI	Opposite Interactions
OPFS	Operational Performance versus Financial Solvency binomial
P	Period of time
QR	Quick Ratio
RB	Gross Sales
SE	Shareholders' Equity
UI	Unidirectional Interactions
VC	Variable cost

Executive Summary

The study of liquidity is a recurring theme in the finance literature that evaluates the nominal payment capacity of organizations, through the quotient of the division of the total sum of liquid assets in cash and assets convertible into cash, by the total sum of obligations, in a time horizon, using an appropriately specified analytical model.

The inputs required by the variables of the model, for the assessment of liquidity, are extracted from the standardized or managerial financial statements of the Economic Agents represented by corporate organizations, civil society organizations and governmental organizations.

This work, derived from theoretical-empirical research, fulfills the purpose of introducing, presenting, developing and testing empirical models that signal and produce evidence that the nominal payment capacity, represented by traditional liquidity rate, such as the current ratio (CR) and general liquidity ratio (GR), is incomplete and needs to combine time rate that match financial cash flow with disbursement and cash disbursement periods, in equivalent time units.

To fulfill the objective of contributing to the literature, discussions about origins and informational content described as characteristics of liquidity, analysis of liquidity properties and necessary and sufficient conditions for liquidity sustainability were developed and are anchors in the research support, and also made possible the introduction with adequate specification of the Financial Efficiency Ratios (FER) and Liquidity Sustainability Ratio (LSR).

The main contributions to the literature, contributed by the research, are the FER and the LSR, which, based on the traditional CR, incorporated the attributes of the activity rate, Operating Cycle (OC) and Financial Cycle (FC), as a proxy for the effective payment capacity or financial solvency, to signal the financial efficiency and sustainable liquidity of organizations.

The theoretical constructs of the FER and the LSR were tested with academic (hypothetical) and market data. The results obtained validate the model because the theoretical assumptions signaled by the metrics of each coefficient were confirmed. Given these confirmations, the contributions to the literature are effective and consistent.

The FER is the rate associated with the interest rate and the quotient of the division of the FC by the OC that signals the financial efficiency of the organization, through a non-linear combination. FER metrics signal whether the organization is financially efficient or financially insufficient

The FER is associated with the CR to obtain the LSR theoretical construct through which the sustainability status of the organization's liquidity is observed. LSR metrics signal whether the organization's liquidity is strongly sustainable or weakly sustainable or not sustainable.

The model tests, with data from 37 firms in the manufacturing sector in Brazil, in the time horizon from 2000 to 2015, reveal that liquidity is poorly sustainable in 77.53% of these firms and that only two firms are financially efficient.

Professor José Antonio de França
University of Brasilia

Professor Wilfredo Sosa Sandoval
Catholic University of Brasilia

Research Plan

Faces of Corporate Liquidity Sustainability - Necessary and Sufficient Conditions - is a technical-analytical content, produced by a theoretical-empirical research, which aims to facilitate the understanding of the informational content of liquidity, as a characteristic of the nominal payment capacity, through the data analysis, structured in four chapters.

Chapter 1

Chapter 1 presents the arguments "financial efficiency" and "current liquidity" as the binomial of the fundamentals of liquidity sustainability that is a proxy for the effective payment capacity or financial solvency of an economic organization.

The informational content of the effective payment capacity is the argument that reports the past and signals the future, diagnosing financial efficiency and sustainable liquidity, as an attribute of the "principle of continuity" that is essential for the maintenance of business and the longevity of the economic organization.

These arguments result from the informational content of the financial statements, prepared in accordance with the accounting standards and practices applicable to transactions and to the specificities of the businesses of economic organizations, over a period of time.

Accounting practices impact the quanta of financial ratios, efficiency ratios and sustainability ratios because they impose recognition of transactions measured at current cost, market value, present value, historical cost and other measurement techniques for the same group of accounts.

The discussion in the chapter shows that these measurement methods effectively have the power to impact the aforementioned ratios, including the indicator that serves as a proxy for liquidity sustainability, but this power does not impact financial solvency because it, financial solvency, is the ability to pay each obligation with cash on hand, that is, the cash inflow cycle occurs before the payment cycle, in sufficient volume to honor each commitment without sacrificing the maturity of other assets.

Finally, the chapter shows a demonstration of the informational content of efficiency, liquidity and sustainability ratios, at points of neutrality or equilibrium, as well as in both directions to the left and right of each ratio, signaling their respective metrics.

Chapter 2

The Chapter 2 addresses the Characteristics of Liquidity: Sources and Information Content. The approach involves modeling current liquidity (short term) and general liquidity (long term), recurrent in the literature. The focus is on the nominal capacity to pay which does not take into account any adjustments to mitigate asymmetries between nominal capacity and effective payment capacity or financial solvency.

The informational content is the characteristic of liquidity that expresses the nominal payment capacity, in the short and long terms, present in Internal Events and External Events, whose constructs were introduced in this chapter.

Internal Events represent the migration of values, with a vertical direction in two directions, on either of the two sides of the balance sheet, assets and liabilities, which impact short-term liquidity and keep long-term liquidity constant, without any transaction between Economic Agents. It is a financial planning scenario for projecting nominal capacity and payment in the short term.

External Events are sustained in horizontal, cross and vertical directions in which there is a relationship between Economic Agents and modify the *quantum* of short-term and long-term liquidity rate. Due to the dynamics of these transactions, the current and liquidity rate.

The origin of liquidity occurs both in the Internal Events scenario and in the External Events scenario and the magnitude of the *quantum* of the liquidity rate depends on the combination of the Event direction with the transaction direction.

In the first scenario, the direction of the migration of values between two balance sheet aggregates determines an increase or decrease in the *quantum* of the liquidity rate. If the direction of migration occurs from Non-Current Assets (NCA) to Current Assets (CA) or from Current Liabilities (CL) to Non-Current Liabilities (NCL), the *quantum* of the liquidity rate increases. If the direction occurs in the opposite direction, the *quantum* decreases.

In the second scenario, the direction of migration only guarantees that there will be an increase or decrease in the *quantum* of the liquidity rate for migration in the cross and vertical directions. In the horizontal direction, there is no such guarantee considering that the transaction value is not proportional to the values of the aggregates involved.

The behavior of the *quanta* of the current liquidity rate, over the time horizon, in the Internal Events scenario, presents indefinite curvature, sometimes concave curvature, sometimes convex curvature. This is because, in the financial planning scenario, the cash requirement changes in each time period.

At the end of the chapter, the conclusions and a QUIZ are presented so that the reader can answer it and assess their understanding of the content covered.

Chapter 3

Chapter 3 analyzes the properties of liquidity with a focus on the short and long terms. The analysis starts from understanding the informational content of Net Working Capital (NWC) and Net Long-Term Capital (NLTC) to predict the meaning of the current liquidity ratio (CR) and the general liquidity ratio (GR) in restricted and comprehensive in horizontal, cross and vertical direction.

The restricted scenario signals the nominal payment capacity, only in a vertical direction, without interaction between Economic Agents, based on any balance sheet aggregate. The magnitude of the quantum of the liquidity indicator is not predictable as it depends on the value of the transaction, and it is only possible to indicate the direction of the shift.

The comprehensive scenario is supported by the interaction between Economic Agents in a horizontal, cross and also vertical direction. In transactions with horizontal direction, the CR *quantum* can increase or decrease, depending on the direction and magnitude of the transaction, considering that the transaction is not proportional to the total of aggregates involved. In the other directions, cross and vertical, the direction follows the flow, and the *quantum* variation follows the magnitude of the transaction.

The nominal payment capacity model, represented by the CR, recurrent in the literature, signals whether an Economic Agent has the means of payment to honor short-term financial commitments, but does not ensure effective payment capacity or financial solvency because it does not associate the *quantum* from the CR the *quanta* of the activity rate represented by the operational cycle (OC) and financial cycle (FC) rate.

The sources for generating nominal payment capacity originate internally and in the prospect of new business. Internal sources, on the asset side of the balance sheet, originate from vertical transactions in the CA aggregate direction, while in the liability side sources, transactions are in the NCL direction. But these sources are already internalized in the informational content of the balance sheet and do not add new business, being used to project the cash flow scenario.

Additional sources of nominal payment capacity generation come from the firm's operational sustainability, measured by the Degree of Operational Leverage (DOL), which signals whether the firm operates at full use of its installed capacity, eliminating waste and idleness.

In the literature review, the most relevant contributions regarding the generation of nominal payment capacity arising from profits and operational leverage are analyzed, as well as the need for informational content that associates the CR with time rate.

Theoretical models are developed that signal the properties of liquidity, in a restricted and comprehensive scenario, with empirical tests using academic (hypothetical) data and market data for model validation.

Finally, the conclusions and a QUIZ are presented to assess the learning of the main topics developed.

Chapter 4

The chapter analyzes an analytical combination of the current liquidity rate (CR) with the financial cycle (FC) and operating cycle (OC) rates, to produce an analytical model of data analysis, which associates the financial efficiency coefficient (FER) to the liquidity sustainability coefficient (LSR). The analytical combination mitigates the effects of the gap in the literature not filled by the CR, such as nominal payment capacity, in the management of financial efficiency and sustainable liquidity, and introduces the necessary and sufficient condition.

The Necessary and Sufficient Condition (NSC) is the argument that supports the theoretical construct of analytical modeling and, based on it, the metrics of financial efficiency and sustainable liquidity that allow data analysis are defined.

The literature review makes use of relevant contributions that demand a consistent rate for liquidity assessment, in addition to the traditional model, which completes the informational content of the CR with the expectations of the cash flow, matching disbursement deadlines with cash disbursement deadlines.

The metrics of the traditional liquidity model are presented, in which the nominal payment capacity, signaled by the CR, reveals strong, weak and insufficient status. The consistency of these metrics depends on compliance with the rules established by accounting for the recognition and measurement of transactions.

The FER model and metrics corroborate the FC model signaling and the firm is financially efficient, strong, if the FER *quantum* is less than 1, which implies that the FC *quantum* is less than zero. If the firm is financially efficient, weak, the FC *quantum* is equal to zero, because the OC and DPO *quanta* are equal. In addition to these two metrics, the firm is financially insufficient because the *quantum* of FC is greater than zero.

The metrics of the LSR model signal that the liquidity status is stratified as strongly sustainable, weakly sustainable and not sustainable. This stratification results from the combination of the CR *quantum*, as a ratio of nominal payment capacity, with the FER *quantum* that defines the financial efficiency status of the firm.

The analysis of the informational content of liquidity sustainability reveals a predominance of firms with unsustainable liquidity status because they have a LSR *quantum* smaller than the CR *quantum* as a consequence of the FER *quantum* being greater than 1.

The informational content of the statistical analysis shows that the status of financial insufficiency is the predominant metric of the FER obtained in the analysis of data from the set of 37 firms in the manufacturing industry in Brazil, in the time horizon from 2000 to 2015, whose data were extracted from the financial statements standardized. This revelation is provided by the reduced *quantum* of the coefficient of variation (CV) estimator close to zero.

Finally, the chapter presents the conclusions and a Quiz to assess the learning of the main topics covered.

Cases and solutions

The research presents three cases with the respective solutions, with the objective of allowing the reader, market professional, professor, researcher and student, to understand the completeness of the work with the desirable conceptual security and adequate application.

Chapter 1

Fundamentals of financial efficiency and liquidity sustainability

Financial efficiency is an argument associated with the sustainability of liquidity. An economic organization is said to be financially efficient if its cash inflows occur before the respective cash outflows and, subsequently, the liquidity of that organization is sustainable if the volume of cash inflows exceeds the volume of cash outflows, at each disbursement, in the chronology of the financial cycle. Otherwise, the economic organization is not financially efficient and does not operate in sustainable liquidity status.

1. Informational content of financial efficiency and sustainable liquidity

Financial efficiency and liquidity, in the corporate world, are sustainability anchors. It is with this understanding that Dunphy and Benveniste (2000) approach liquidity as a concept that prolongs the life of organizations. So, financial efficiency and liquidity can be understood as a necessary and sufficient condition (NSC) for financial balance because they are a relevant requirement for the continuity of the organization, as they are the foundation of financial solvency, as De França and Sandoval (2019) argue when introducing the financial efficiency ratio (FER) and the liquidity sustainability ratio (LSR). In this condition, financial solvency is an argument for sustainable liquidity.

An economic organization with financial solvency status is a financially efficient organization. So, sustainability of liquidity requires, simultaneously, the arguments of financial efficiency and financial solvency.

Sustainability is the "continuity principle" argument. If an Economic Agent meets the requirements of financial efficiency and liquidity, that Economic Agent operates in a financially efficient and sustainable liquidity context. This association is imperative because it reflects the combination of time variables, such as the financial cycle, with the economic variable of nominal payment capacity measured by the current ratio (CR), as the main financial ratio of current liquidity. From now on, the terminologies current liquidity ratio or liquidity ratio have the same semantics, and Economic Organization and Economic Agent are also semantically equivalent.

So, sustainability is a prescription recited, on a recurring basis, not only in terms of financial liquidity, but also in various segments of human existence, such as ecology, social relations and the economy. In ecology, the prescription reiterates the care with fauna (animals), flora (vegetation), waters and other biomes so that the planet's balance is maintained. In social relationships, the focus is on respect, resilience, tolerance and non-violence so that people's lives and between people are constructive and civilized. In the economy, the motivation is the prosperity obtained through production, the distribution of wealth, social balance and human dignity. Thus, for these segments of society, sustainability is like the *mantra* for *Hinduism* in which balance is, at the same time, a sign of cause and effect of sustainable practices.

Practices are sustainable if they are incorporated into the organizational culture and if they are part of the business strategy, and not just contained in a periodic report to meet normative and superficial requirements, as Hawkins (2006) addresses. This context requires commitment and delivery of what is committed because it implies credibility, such as, for example, delivering what sells with the promised quality, respecting contractual rules and building partnerships, because business management revolves around customers and partners who are liquidity management links.

The context of liquidity management requires observation of nominal payment capacity and effective payment capacity. The nominal ability to pay is impacted by accounting standards that regulate procedures to recognize and measure assets and liabilities, but these procedures may not ensure financial solvency, as addressed by Moir (1997), because if payment dates do not occur after the due dates of cash inflow there will be no funds to settle the obligations and, in this case, it is necessary to resort to alternative financial contributions. Effective payment capacity ensures financial solvency because it ensures that for each cash disbursement date there are sufficient funds to honor the financial commitments.

The arguments presented in this discussion are supported by the informational content of the data disclosed by economic organizations in their financial statements. These financial statements are prepared following the guidance of accounting standards oriented by regulators for various business segments, with their respective specificities. These specifics report the economic organization's operating segment for regulated or unregulated business.

These accounting standards can influence the magnitude of the volume of nominal payment capacity because of transaction recognition estimates that, at one point in a time horizon, can further impact the *quantum* of the current liquidity ratio and at another point can impact this *quantum* to less, without any impact on the measure of financial solvency. In this context, it is evident that the current liquidity ratio is nothing more than a nominal payment capacity ratio whose *quantum* depends on the movement and direction of the accounting estimates.

Accounting estimates introduce uncertainties in the magnitude of liquidity as a sign of nominal payment capacity. These uncertainties may result from market signals regarding changes in the economic scenario, the political scenario or any other scenario that may impact the financial solvency conditions of organizations. The procedures for recognizing the effects of these changes are regulated by accounting standards to produce the estimates materialized in the financial statements of organizations that are the source of data for analyzing the fundamentals of financial efficiency and liquidity sustainability.

The analysis of liquidity, for whatever the scenario, optimistic or not optimistic, starts from the informational content of the organizations' financial statements. It is important to note that this informational content, for calculating the liquidity ratio, refers to the past with an impact on the future, which is the business continuity scenario. Thus, it is important to assess whether these acts allow the organization to satisfy the requirements of the "principle of continuity", such as being sustainable, in the context of the triple-bottom-line or three Ps: people, planet and profit, as defended by Elkington (1997).

The informational content of liquidity signals sustainability, as a passport to the future, and consequently continuity, if this content is guaranteed by financial efficiency so that the economic organization is financially solvent. This guarantee will be long-lasting and will be sustained as the governance of the economic organization is committed to the fiduciary responsibility of preserving social, ecological and economic relationships to mitigate inherent risks of the business.

2. What characterizes an organization's sustainability?

In the approach of this liquidity context research, an organization is sustainable if it fulfills its obligations to customers, suppliers, investors and other stakeholders, keeping them satisfied with the present business and confident in the future business. In other words, it is the fulfillment of duties and mission in the short term that allows achieving the goals of continuity in the long term, with sustainable profitability and liquidity.

In the approach of Dyllick and Hockerts (2002) a sustainable organization must consider, in addition to economic aspects, social and environmental aspects because there is an interdependence between them that involves stock of financial capital, natural capital, human and social capital. Similarly, Zink, Steimle and Fischer (2008) argue that economic systems are continuously modeled and that this modeling is the characteristic that allows the organization to understand and adapt to the "principle of continuity" to serve future generations, because corporate sustainability it must satisfy the economic-financial demands associated with the environmental and social demands in the set of common business objectives.

Exploring a contemporary line of thinking Szekely and Dossa (2017) discuss the meaning of the sustainable mission of a home appliance manufacturing organization, detailing it in four phases. **Phase 1**: survival; **Phase 2**: environmentalism; **Phase 3**: social responsibility; and **Phase 4**: sustainability. They detail survival as the need to stay of business, environmentalism as the silent inclusion of the "environment" stakeholder, social responsibility as the promotion of happy and healthy homes, and sustainability as the responsibility to improve people's lives through transformative home solutions.

Other research on sustainability, in a comprehensive way, is available in the literature, including on the sustainability of liquidity sustained in financial efficiency, as De França and Sandoval (2019) did when introducing the concept and model of coefficients that signal a financially efficient firm with sustainable liquidity.

So, the sustainability of an organization, in terms of liquidity management, is not restricted to comfortable ratios of current liquidity, but it is necessary to meet the other requirements of respect for social and environmental rules that preserve life, fairly remunerate the investment, with profit generation, because it is this set of interdependent practices, of solutions, that will guarantee the continuity of the business.

3. Impact of accounting practices on the information content of liquidity

The economic-financial informational content of economic organizations is publicly known through the disclosure of financial statements prepared in accordance with current accounting standards and practices. For each economic organization, even if under the same guidance, the practices are applied according to the specifics of transactions and the organization's business. Thus, accounting practices impact the informational content of financial statements and indicate the magnitude of liquidity in a given time horizon.

These accounting practices arising from the guidelines aim at the recognition of transactions, on a timely basis and by estimate, at historical cost, current price, market price or another form of evaluation applicable to the nature of the transaction. Examples of these transactions are inventories valued at cost or sale price, receivables reduced by default risk, financial assets and liabilities valued at present value, etc.

The *quantum* of the liquidity indicator, resulting from these practices, is impacted by the estimates, without any change in the financial solvency as a result of the increase or reduction of the effective payment capacity. Therefore, this quantum only signals nominal payment capacity and is dependent on the respective accounting practices. In this context, if accounting practices are adequate, the information content of the liquidity indicator is fair, otherwise, the ratio may be biased and compromise decision making.

Accounting practices modify the informational content of liquidity because they impact the balances of financial and non-financial assets, as well as with regard to financial and non-financial liabilities.

The recognition of estimates of financial assets and liabilities, including sales receivables and obligations with suppliers, as well as the recognition of estimates of non-financial assets, including sales inventories, have the power to impact the financial efficiency ratio (FER) because they change activity, operational cycle (OC) and financial cycle (FC) indicators; impacts the current liquidity ratio (CR) and liquidity sustainability ratio (LSR) because they are variables of the algebraic combination of proxy estimation that signals effective liquidity, as specified in chapter 4 further on.

Figure 1 shows the meaning of the quanta of the FER, CR and LSR ratios that are the basis for the interpretation of the informational content of the financial statements of economic organizations. The FER quantum equal to 1 signals a neutral position of financial efficiency, but still efficient, being insufficient on the right and 1 and efficient on the left of 1. The CR quantum equal to 1, suggests balance between assets and obligations to be honored with these assets, financial and non-financial, in short term, being insufficient to the left of 1 and sufficient to the right of 1. Finally, the LSR uses, as a reference, the CR quantum to display the quantum of the effective payment capacity. If the CR and LSR *quanta* are equal, the CR represents, simultaneously, the nominal and effective payment capacities. Otherwise, liquidity will be strongly sustainable for CR, at least, equal to 1 positioned to the left of the LSR, and weakly sustainable liquidity for CR, at least, equal to 1 positioned to the right of the LSR.

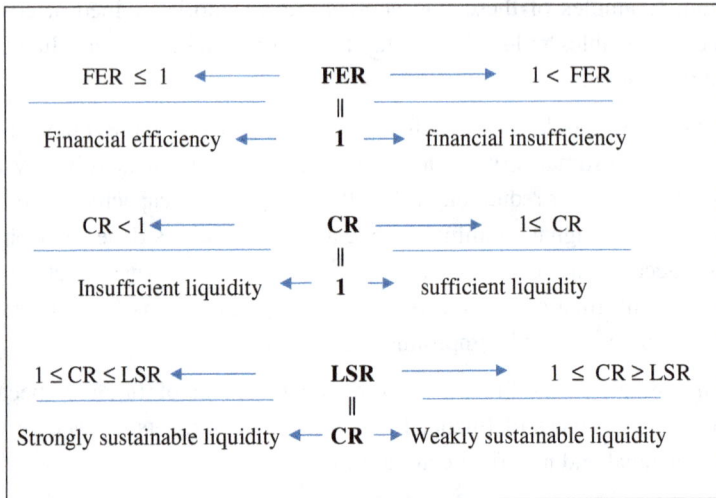

$FER \leq 1 \longleftarrow$ $FER \longrightarrow$ $1 < FER$

$\parallel$

Financial efficiency $\longleftarrow$ $1 \longrightarrow$ financial insufficiency

$CR < 1 \longleftarrow$ $CR \longrightarrow$ $1 \leq CR$

$\parallel$

Insufficient liquidity $\longleftarrow$ $1 \longrightarrow$ sufficient liquidity

$1 \leq CR \leq LSR \longleftarrow$ $LSR \longrightarrow$ $1 \leq CR \geq LSR$

$\parallel$

Strongly sustainable liquidity $\longleftarrow$ $CR \longrightarrow$ Weakly sustainable liquidity

Figure 1: Metrics of efficiency, liquidity and sustainability indicators arising from accounting practices

4. Conclusions

The approach in this chapter has shown that liquidity, anchored in the fundamentals of financial efficiency, is a relevant instrument for managing sustainability, as it represents the effective payment capacity as a proxy for financial solvency.

The discussion indicated that the liquidity ratios are impacted by the estimates of recognition and measurement of economic transactions, guided by accounting practices and standards and that they, the practices and standards, also impact the informational content of the financial statements, prepared by Economic Agents, which are the basis of the informational content of the liquidity ratios.

Finally, the chapter also demonstrated, with graphic resources, the meaning of the FER, CR and LSR ratios, as ratios of sustainable liquidity and financial efficiency of an Economic Agent, signaling the informational content of each ratio, to the left and right of the its reference *quantum*.

References

De França, J.A. & Sandoval, W.S. (2019). Necessary and Sufficient Conditions for Liquidity Management. International Journal of Economics and Finance. V.11, nr. 5.

Dunphy, Dexter and Benveniste, Jodie (2000). Sustainability: the corporate challenge of the 21st century. (Uma introdução à corporação sustentável). Australia. Allen & Unwin.

Dyllick, Thomas; HockertS, Kai. (2002). Beyond the business case for corporate sustainability. Business Strategy and the Environment. v. 11, n.2, p.130-141, Mar/Apr.

Elkington, John. (1997). Cannibals with forks: the triple bottom Line of 21st Century Business. Oxford. Capstone.

Hawkins, David E. (2006). Corporate Social Responsibility (Balancing tomorrow's sustainability and today's profitability). New York Palgrave Macmillan.

Moir, Lance. (1997). Managing Liquidity. 2th. Ed. Cambridge. Woodhead.

Szekely, Francisco and Dossa, Zahir. (2017). Beyond the Triple Bottom Line: Eight Steps toward a Sustainable Business Model.U.S.A. MIT Press.

Zink, Klaus J.; Steimle, Ulrich e Fischer, Klaus. (2008). Corporate Sustainability as a Challenge for Comprehensive Management (Human Factors, Business Excellence and Corporate Sustainability: Differing Perspectives, Joint Objectives). Germany. Physica-Verlag.

Chapter 2

Liquidity Characteristics: origins and informational content

This chapter addresses aspects of corporate liquidity measured by the current liquidity ratio (CR) and general liquidity ratio (GR) models as they are diffusely known in the literature. The approach is centered on the characteristics, origin and informational content of liquidity supported by concepts and attributes associated with Internal Events and External Events that relate the balance sheet aggregates to define the nominal payment capacity of an Economic Agent, at a given point of a time horizon.

1. Liquidity Characteristics

The balance sheet aggregates that define the nominal payment capacity of an Economic Agent are classified as Current Assets (CA), Non-Current Assets (NCA), Current Liabilities (CL) and Non-Current Liabilities (NCL). This classification follows the guidance of the IFRS (International Financial Reporting Standards) edited by the IASB Foundation (International Accounting Standards Board) which defines the layout of the balance sheet standard disclosed to external users of the information. From these balance sheet aggregates, liquidity ratios are obtained, based on diffuse models in the literature, from which informational content is obtained as a characteristic or attribute of liquidity.

Based on this structured information, the chapter introduces the characteristics of liquidity based on origins and informational content. The origins are signaled by the Internal Events and External Events constructs, whose measurement attribute is quantitative. The informational content is the liquidity characteristic that expresses the nominal payment capacity. Economic Agent is the name used to designate a firm, a civil society organization and a governmental organization. From this paragraph onwards, Economic Agent and firm will be used as analogous terminologies.

The nominal payment capacity is presented in the short term and in the long term through the current liquidity ratio (CR) and the general liquidity ratio (GR), respectively, which must be evaluated in a comparative view between the sum of assets in cash with assets to be converted into cash and the sum of liabilities payable in cash. The CR as a short-term ratio is observed in a time interval between two balance sheets or between two consecutive fiscal years, while the GR, as a long-term ratio, is observed from the CR.

The comparative view of liquidity, as a nominal payment capacity, is a heterogeneous view, albeit temporal, because it does not associate the disbursement dates with the disbursement dates to match the punctuality of the inflows and outflows of financial resources that make up the cash flow of the Economic Agent. Therefore, the informational content of the nominal ability to pay differs from the informational content of the effective ability to pay, as shown in Chapter 4.

The Internal Events construct shows how liquidity, representing the nominal payment capacity, is generated and changes based on the migration of values between balance sheet aggregates. If the direction of migration is from the NCA aggregate to the CA aggregate or from the CL aggregate to the NCL aggregate, this migration has a vertical direction and implies an increase in the CR *quantum*, but does not impact the GR *quantum*. On the other hand, if the direction of migration is from CA to NCA or from NCL to CL, the impact is a reduction in the CR *quantum* and, as in the previous migration, the GR *quantum* does not change. Now, if the migration only occurs within the same aggregate, the impact on CR and NCL *quanta* is null.

The External Events construct displays the dynamics of liquidity from the interaction between Economic Agents, in carrying out transactions with horizontal or cross direction on opposite sides of the balance sheet or even with vertical direction involving at least two aggregates on the same side of the balance sheet so that there is a change in at least one liquidity ratio.

Transactions in a horizontal direction are those that involve CA and CL, NCA and NCL, Fixed Assets (FA) and Equity on the balance sheet of an Economic Agent, simultaneously, regardless of which side of the balance sheet is the aggregate that gives rise to the transaction.

Transactions in the cross direction are those that start from an aggregate on one side of the balance sheet (assets or liabilities) and involve other aggregates on the other side of the balance sheet (assets or liabilities) in a diagonal direction. If the transaction originates in asset-side aggregates, the meanings are as follows: (a) from CA to NCL and Equity; (b) from NCA to CL and Equity; (c) from FA to CL and NCL. For transactions initiated on the liability side, the directions are: (d) from CL to NCA and FA; (e) from NCL to CA and FA; (f) from Equity to CA and NCA.

Transactions in a vertical direction, in External Events, are those caused by the interaction of the Economic Agent with other agents that involve one or more aggregates on the same side of the balance sheet, and transactions within the same aggregate do not impact liquidity ratios.

The chapter also presents metrics from the liquidity models, CA and GR, indicating the respective restrictions, as well as demonstrating, in the Cartesian plane (Figure 9 at the end of this chapter), that the CA curve resulting from Internal Events has a non-concave behavior and that the GR is constant due to the fact that that the sums of CA and NCA and of CL and NCL do not change. However, the behavior of the curve depends on the magnitude of the ratio *quantum*.

Regarding the *quanta* of the ratios, CR and GR, revealed in the empirical tests of the model, they were obtained with hypothetical data from academic simulations, considering that this internal migration of values between balance sheet aggregates is not available in the information for external users disclosed in the balance sheets of firms, but that this way of testing does not invalidate the results.

So, based on these assumptions, the effectiveness of an Economic Agent in honoring its financial commitments depends on the quality of its financial liquidity, such as nominal payment capacity, measured in a time horizon defined between two balance sheets or between two consecutive fiscal years, when dealing with short-term liquidity or beyond that time horizon when dealing with long-term liquidity.

The financial liquidity of an Economic Agent is one of the relevant topics that make up the study of corporate finance, characterized as nominal payment capacity, which evolves into effective payment capacity or financial solvency. Thus, the informational content of the nominal payment capacity is a relevant characteristic of a liquidity ratio.

This characteristic, informational content of the nominal payment capacity, object of the liquidity ratio, when considered in the short term, is the quotient resulting from the division of the sum of financial assets with non-monetary assets, classified in CA, by the total of obligations classified in CL, both convertible and payable in currency, within a time horizon between two balance sheets or between two consecutive fiscal years. When liquidity is considered in the long term, the CA is added to the NCA and to the CL is added the NCL. In this context, the nominal capacity to pay is a comparative view between the sum of assets in cash with assets to be converted into cash and the sum of liabilities payable in cash, at a point in the same time horizon.

The comparative view, observed in this way, is valid for the defined time interval, but it does not associate the concomitant dates of cash inflow and cash outflow contemplated in the Economic Agent's cash flow, and this makes it a heterogeneous view because it can signal that, within the defined period of time, liquidity would be satisfactory, but not in a timely manner, because it does not match the dates of cash outflows with the dates of cash inflows, and there may not be enough cash to honor all the commitments in the required time. Thus, in this scenario, the Economic Agent would have liquidity but would not be financially solvent, as discussed by Richards and Laughlin (1980); Lancaster, Stevens and Jennings (1998); Sharifi and Taghipour (2014); and De França & Sandoval (2019). This heterogeneity is placed as a restriction on nominal liquidity in relation to the effective liquidity or financial solvency of the Economic Agent.

The heterogeneity, as observed, is motivated by the incompatibility of cash disbursement and disbursement dates that qualitatively restrict the informational content of liquidity ratio, and may even disqualify them as ratios of effective payment capacity or financial solvency, because an Economic Agent may present satisfactory liquidity but not be financially capable of honoring financial commitments, due to insufficient cash. This anomalous situation occurs when the cash outflow dates precede the cash inflow dates, causing cash insufficiency, even if the nominal liquidity ratio is robust.

Liquidity, as an instrument of financial management of the Economic Agent, represented by indices obtained with the use of balance sheet aggregates, is defined by the ratios **(a)** Acid Test Ratio (AT), **(b)** Quick Ratio (QR), **(c)** Current Ratio (CR), and **(d)** General Ratio (GR).

The AT ratio restricts liquidity to the ratio of available financial resources in cash and cash equivalents to total short-term liabilities. The QR promotes the relaxation of the restriction imposed by the AT because it adds to the assets in cash and equivalents the assets represented by receivables in the short term and compares the sum of these assets with the total liabilities payable in the short term. The CR further relaxes this constraint because it considers the sum of all cash and cash equivalents and other assets convertible into cash, in the short term, with the total liabilities payable in cash in the short term, in the interval between two balance sheets or two consecutive fiscal years.

The GR, being a less accurate ratio due to the lengthening of time, relaxes all these restrictions because it compares the total of balance sheet aggregates, realizable in the short and long term, with the total of aggregates payable in the short and long term.

Taking into account the restrictions of the AT and the QR, the ratios considered in the study of this chapter are only the CR and GR, because they incorporate the informational content of the first two, whose analytical models are presented later.

The denominations "short-term" and "long-term" are used to indicate that a transaction must be recognized in a Current Assets CA account or in a Non-Current Assets (NCA) account, respectively, as well as in a Current Liabilities account (CL) and in the Non-Current Liabilities (NCL) account, depending on the maturity of the right or obligation. Thus, in the accounting literature, a transaction that is expected to generate cash inflows within one year or in the course of a fiscal year is considered short-term and recognized in Current Assets. On the other hand, a transaction that is expected to generate cash disbursements within one year or in the course of a fiscal year is recognized as Current Liabilities. Otherwise, for both transactions, recognition is done in NCA and NCL, as long-term transactions.

This recognition of transactions in the balance sheet aggregates CA, NCA, CL and NCL, depending on the term, is a rule emanating from the normative acts of the IFRS (International Financial Reporting Standards) standard edited by the IASB Foundation (International Accounting Standards Board) so that there is comparability between the information disclosed in the balance sheets of Economic Agents.

The CR is a ratio that originates from the dynamics of the Economic Agent's working capital, by comparing the CA with the CL. In this sense, the CR is a relevant ratio to signal the behavior of financial management considering two scenarios called Internal Events and External Events, as will be discussed in the next section of this chapter. But it is important to make it clear from now on that the two scenarios are not competing scenario only, because the Internal Events signals how the nominal payment capacity behaves, in the face of a financial planning scenario to strengthen the Economic Agent's cash, in a fixed point of time, while External Events report the dynamics and continuity of the business, with the inherent risks.

2. Origins of liquidity

Nominal liquidity originates from Internal Events and External Events. Each event has specific characteristics. Internal Events are characterized by the migration or displacement of values between different aggregates on the same balance sheet side, in a vertical direction, without modifying the joint sum of the aggregates involved. External Events are a consequence of the natural dynamics of businesses that operate in a horizontal or cross or vertical direction and therefore can impact the nominal payment capacity signaled by the CR and the GR.

The vertical direction exerted by Internal Events in a transaction can increase or decrease CA and NCA simultaneously, just as it does with respect to NCL or CL. This movement also contributes to increasing or decreasing short-term liquidity measured by the CR *quantum* because the value that increases in one aggregate is equal to the value that decreases in the other aggregate. In this way, this movement, regardless of which side of the balance it occurs, does not change the joint sum of the balance sheet aggregates and, as a consequence, the GR *quantum* remains constant because the movement is in the same direction, but in opposite movements, as long as one of the aggregates involved is not Fixed Assets or Net Equity.

External Events are exercised by the interaction between Economic Agents, in transactions with a horizontal or cross or even vertical direction. If the transaction has a horizontal or cross direction, it changes the sum of the individual aggregates on each side of the balance in non-proportional amounts and, as a consequence, affects the CR *quanta* and may affect the GR *quantum*. But if the transaction in External Events is with vertical direction, it does not impact the GR *quantum* if it occurs within the same aggregate. Otherwise, CR and GR *quanta* may be impacted depending on the amount of aggregates involved in the transaction.

Internal Events. Internal Events, if on the asset side of the balance sheet, increase or decrease CA, as they do with NCA in the same magnitude of value, if the transaction does not involve FA. If on the liability side of the balance sheet, they increase or reduce CL or NCL, if they do not involve Equity. In this way, the displacement of value in the movement of this event, regardless of which side of the balance sheet it occurs, does not change the joint sum of the balance sheet aggregates, if the transaction is restricted to short-term aggregates, a situation in which the *quantum* of the GR remains constant. Otherwise, if FA or Equity is involved, the GR *quantum* will be impacted or jointly the CR and GR *quanta* will be impacted. This movement occurs due to the reallocation of values from one balance sheet aggregate to another, depending on the maturity of a right or obligation or even the need for internal financing. This dynamic occurs without interaction between Economic Agents to design liquidity management scenarios.

External Events. External Events change the *quantum* of liquidity ratios from the interaction between Economic Agents because the direction of these events can be horizontal or cross on opposite sides of the balance sheet, or even vertical on the same side of the balance sheet. However, there are External Events that do not change liquidity because they may be vertical transactions that involve only an aggregate on the same side of the balance sheet, such as, for example, the split of an already recognized obligation to more than one creditor or a right to more than one debtor, provided they remain within the limits of the same balance sheet aggregate. Typical cases of External Events that involve vertical transactions between Economic Agents, which do not change liquidity, are, on the asset side, **(a)** bank deposits of cash and **(b)** cash inflow for redemption of receivables. On the liability side, it can be considered **(a)** segregation of creditors by consignment in which the Economic Agent is authorized to pay a debt for the account and order of another and **(b)** incidence of withholding taxation on the purchase of goods and services that must the segregation of the tax obligation occurs from the recognition of the obligation.

A transaction with vertical direction, promoted by Internal Events or by External Events, does not change the *quantum* of the liquidity ratio if it occurs within the limits of the same balance sheet aggregate, either on the asset or liability side. Otherwise, the *quantum* of the liquidity ratio will change, up or down, depending on the direction of the transaction.

Thus, confirming, in a cross transaction, there will always be a modification of the liquidity ratio because at least two balance sheet aggregates, one on each side, in a diagonal direction, which is related to the nominal payment capacity, will be affected.

3. CR dynamics and GR statics in the context of Internal Events

Figures 2 to 9 show the dynamics of the CR, from the migration of values between the balance sheet aggregates, in the composition of the nominal payment capacity. In figures 2 to 6 and 8, the flow direction is vertical, represented by arrows, with displacements in three directions. **(a)** this direction ⇑ indicates increase in value in the short-term aggregate and decrease in value in the long-term aggregate, **(b)** this direction ⇓ indicates increase in value in the long-term aggregate and reduction in value in the short-term aggregate, **(c)** these opposite movements ↑↓ indicate flow in the vertical direction.

Figure 2 shows a transaction that migrates value from NCA to CA (↑). This migration promotes growth in the CR *quantum* because it transfers values from the long term to the short term, but the CL and NCL aggregates remain constant and, therefore, the GR *quantum* does not change, remaining constant.

Balance Sheet Aggregates	Movement	CR	GR
Current assets (CA)			
↑	⇑		
Non-Current Assets (NCA)		Increase	Constant
Current Liabilities (CL)	Constant		
Non-Current Liabilities (NCL)	Constant		

Figure 2: Transactions with vertical direction from NCA to CA with constant CL and NCL

Figure 3 shows the migration of value in the opposite direction to Figure 2, reducing the value of the aggregate CA and increasing the value of the aggregate NCA (↓), in the same magnitude of value. The flow direction promotes reduction (decreases) of the CR *quantum*, but as the CL and NCL aggregates remain constant, the GR *quantum* does not change, it remains constant. This migration of value reduces cash expectations and should be part of the Economic Agent's financial strategy.

Balance Sheet Aggregates	Movement	CR	GR
Current assets (CA)			
↓			
Non-Current Assets (NCA)	⇓		
		Decrease	Constant
Current Liabilities (CL)	Constant		
Non-Current Liabilities (NCL)	Constant		

Figure 3: Transactions with vertical direction from CA to NCA with constant CL and NCL

Unlike figures 2 and 3, now, in figures 4 and 5, the migration of values is restricted to the balance sheet CL and NCL aggregates, keeping the CA and

NCA aggregates constant. The dynamics on the asset side of the balance sheet, within the Economic Agent's strategy, signals the opportunity to convert into cash with more or less time, while the dynamics on the liability side signals the preservation of cash for as long as possible.

Figure 4 shows the migration of value from the NCL aggregate to the CL aggregate ($\uparrow$). This shift in value puts pressure on cash outflows because it increases short-term liabilities. Thus, this migration $\Uparrow$ reduces the CR *quantum* because the CA does not change and the CL grows in value. As the CA and NCA aggregates remain constant, the GR quantum does not change and remains constant.

Balance Sheet Aggregates	Movement	CR	GR
Current assets (CA)	constant		
Non-Current Assets (NCA)	constant		
		Decrease	Constant
Current Liabilities (CL)			
$\uparrow$	$\Uparrow$		
Non-Current Liabilities (NCL)			

Figure 4: Transactions with vertical direction from NCL to CL with constant CA and NCA

Finally, in **Figure 5**, the migration of value is in the opposite movement to that of Figure 4, promoting a reduction in the aggregate CL ($\downarrow$) and increasing the aggregate NCL ($\uparrow$). This migration $\Downarrow$ relieves pressure on cash because it reduces the outlay for rolling over the debt. The effect of migration in the opposite movement to Figure 4 is the increase in the CR *quantum* because the CL decreases in value. So, this movement also keeps the GR *quantum* unchanged.

Balance Sheet Aggregates	Movement	CR	GR
Current assets (CA)	Constant		
Non-Current Assets (NCA)	Constant		
		Increase	Constant
Current Liabilities (CL)			
$\downarrow$	$\Downarrow$		
Non-Current Liabilities (NCL)			

Figure 5: Transactions with vertical direction from CL to NCL with constant CA and NCA

In summary, the Internal Events approach shows that the nominal payment capacity measured by the CR signals that, in the absence of a change in the total realizable assets and liabilities, the dynamics of the CR depends exclusively on the cash management of assets already recognized to solve obligations already assumed. This scenario, Internal Events, is a financial scenario projection to help understand the source of liquidity and the preservation of corporate finances in strategic financial planning.

4. The dynamics of the CR and the GR in the context of External Events

In External Events, unlike Internal Events, there is interaction between Economic Agents involving transactions with horizontal direction, cross direction on opposite sides of the balance sheet. Transactions with vertical direction may also occur on the same side of the balance sheet as a result of maturity and/or split of rights and obligations.

Transaction with horizontal direction. An economic transaction, in a horizontal direction, impacts the *quantum* of the current liquidity ratio, CR, if it modifies the total value of the balance sheet aggregates, CA and CL. If the totals of the CA and CL aggregates are changed by the same magnitude of value, then the CR *quantum* is reduced if the total value of the two aggregates increases. Otherwise, if the total value of the two aggregates decreases, the CR *quantum* increases.

Figure 6 shows the transaction direction and flow represented by the two arrows [⇆] signaling the two movements of value migration. The transaction with horizontal direction simultaneously changes two balance sheet aggregates on opposite sides.

Balance Sheet Aggregates (Assets)	Moviment	Balance Sheet Aggregates (Liabilities)	CA	GR
Current Assets (CA)	⇆	Current Liabilities (CL)	↑↓	↑↓
Non-Current Assets (NCA)	⇆	Non-Current Liabilities (NCL)	↑↓	↑↓
Fixed Assets (FA)	⇆	Net Equity (NE)	Constant	Constant

Figure 6: Horizontal transactions between aggregates on different sides of the balance sheet

Transaction with cross **direction**. A cross transaction changes at least one aggregate on each side of the balance sheet that relates to the nominal capacity to pay, either in the short term or in the long term, unlike a horizontal transaction that always changes two aggregates, one on each opposite side of the balance sheet.

Figure 7 shows the cross direction and flow (set of arrows) that signal the direction of each transaction. Each transaction changes, at least, one aggregate of the nominal payment capacity.

Balance Sheet Aggregates (Assets)	Moviment	Balance Sheet Aggregates (Liabilities)	CA	GR
Current Assets (CA)		Current Liabilities (CL)	↑↓	↑↓
Non-Current Assets (NCA)		Non-Current Liabilities (NCL)	↑↓	↑↓
Fixed Assets (FA)		Net Equity (NE)	↑↓	↑↓

Figure 7: Cross transactions between aggregates from different sides of the balance sheet

Transaction with vertical direction. Similar to an Internal Event, an External Event with vertical direction within the same balance sheet aggregate does not change the aggregate sum and therefore does not modify the *quantum* of the liquidity ratio. The *quantum* of the liquidity ratio changes if the transaction involves more than one aggregate on the same side of the balance sheet, as shown in Figures 8(a) and 8(b).

Figure 8(a) shows transactions with a vertical direction between all aggregates on the asset side of the balance sheet, in which the flows represented by the arrows, in double direction, indicate the migration of values. The CR is impacted in the transaction involving CA and NCA, but is not impacted in the transaction involving NCA and FA. GR is impacted in the transaction involving NCA and FA, but not in the transaction between CA and NCA. Both the CR and the GR are simultaneously impacted in the transaction between the CA and the FA.

Balance Sheet Aggregates (Assets)	Moviment	CR	GR	CR	CR	GR
Current Assets (CA)		↑↓ Change. CA, NCA	↑↓ No Change. CA, NCA	No Change. FA NCA	↑↓ Change FA CA	↑↓ Change. AF CA, NCA
Non-Current Assets (NCA)						
Fixed Assets (FA)						

Figure 8(a): Transactions with vertical direction between aggregates on the asset side of the balance sheet

Figure 8(b) reports transactions with vertical direction between aggregates on the liability side of the balance sheet. The transaction involving CL and NCL keeps the joint sum of the two aggregates unchanged, impacting the CR, but the GR is not impacted. Conversely, the transaction involving SE (Equity) and NCL does not impact the CR, but it does with respect to the GR. On the other hand, the transaction involving CL and SE (Equity), simultaneously, impacts the CR and the GR.

Balance Sheet Aggregates (Liabilities)	Moviment	CR	GR	CR	CR	GR
Current Liabilities (CL)		↑↓ Change. CL, NCL	↑↓ No change. CL, NCL	No change. SE NCL	↑↓ Change. SE CL	↑↓ Change SE CL, NCL
Non-Current Liabilities (NCL)						
Shareholders' Equity (SE)						

Figure 8(b): Transactions with vertical direction between aggregates on the liability side of the balance sheet

5. Informational content of liquidity ratios

As already stated in previous parts of this chapter, the informational content of liquidity ratio is the main characteristic of liquidity as a nominal payment capacity. This nominal payment capacity, from the point of view of corporate finance, is the starting point for analyzing the effective payment capacity or financial solvency of the Economic Agent. The conceptual approach of Internal Events and External Events of liquidity has also been made, and examples are introduced for data analysis based on them.

5.1 The CR and GR models and informational content

The analytical models of CR and GR are recurrent in the literature and can be found in most specialized publications. However, it is important to note that in the balance sheet of an Economic Agent there may be an asset that does not meet the conditions for conversion into cash, as well as there may be a liability that does not require a cash requirement. In these two situations the corresponding aggregates must be adjusted to mitigate the bias of the ratios. Inequalities (1) and (2) show the calculation model of the CR and the GR with signaling of the restrictions imposed on each of the models, which is the denominator being greater than zero.

$$CR_t = \frac{CA_t}{CL_t} \geq 1, \forall\ CL > 0 \qquad (1)$$

$$GR_t = \frac{CA_t + NCA_t}{CL_t + NCL_t} \geq 1, \qquad \forall\ (CL + NCL) > 0 \qquad (2)$$

Even if these two analytical liquidity models are properly specified, the information content of each one of them will depend on compliance with accounting rules, in the recognition and allocation of asset and liability values that make up the aggregates that support the calculation. Otherwise, the informational content of these ratios may not produce information to meet the decision-making process. So, compliance with each ratio being at least equal to 1 is the informational content required for comfort in decision making.

5.2 CR and GR informational content in the context of Internal Events

The analytical approach with hypothetical data shown in Table 1 is centered on the CR and GR ratios, in the context of Internal Events, in which there is no interaction between Economic Agents. The data show the effect of migration with vertical direction between the aggregates CA and NCA, on the active side, and between CL and NCL, on the liability side. This migration results in an increase or reduction in the nominal payment capacity, in the short term, following the movement of the migration of transactions.

The CR increases in T2 and T3, decreases in T4, increases in T5 and decreases again in T6. This occurs because the total of the aggregate CA is increasing in the times T2, T3, it is constant in T4, it decreases in T5 and in T6, while the total of the aggregate CL is constant in the first three times (T), it increases in T4, it decreases at T5 and grows back at T6. As the characteristic of Internal

Events is not to change the joint total sum of the aggregates CA and NCA, on the asset side, and CL and NCL on the liability side, the GR remains constant.

The CR is sensitive to the variation of the CA and CL aggregates because it is the quotient of the division of the first aggregate by the second aggregate, as shown in Equation 1 previous. Thus, the CR *quantum* increases when migration occurs in the NCA → CA movement and the CL remains constant, or when the migration occurs in the CL → NCL movement and the CA remains constant.

So, the sum of the CA aggregates with NCA, and the CL aggregates with NCL, is always constant because the scenario is of Internal Events and in this scenery there is no interaction between the Economic Agent and other agents. These scenery are relevant to simulate financial planning alternatives, as discussed by Myers (1984), when he addresses the first priority in the Pecking Order Theory (POT) hierarchy, in which the Economic Agent first resorts to internal sources and then launches itself to other alternatives.

Regarding the GR, its *quantum* is constant in all six T periods because the sums of total assets and liabilities are constant, but distinct, and this also confirms the Internal Events characteristic of the origin of liquidity in keeping the GR *quantum* constant. For the purposes of the example in Table 1, the other balance sheet account aggregates were omitted because the transactions in the scenario are restricted to the CA, NCA, CL and NCL aggregates. On the other hand, it is clear that the other two liquidity models, AT and QR, because they are contained in the two models CR and GR, are not addressed in this study.

Table 1: Origin of liquidity - Internal Events - horizon of 6 time periods (T)

ASSETS	T1	T2	T3	T4	T5	T6
Current Assets	**46.600**	**48.600**	**52.600**	**52.600**	**49.600**	**44.600**
Cash and Equivalents	5.500	5.500	7.500	7.500	7.500	7.500
Accounts Receivable	15.600	17.600	17.600	17.600	17.600	17.600
Inventory	20.800	20.800	20.800	20.800	20.800	15.800
Short Term Investments	4.700	4.700	6.700	6.700	3.700	3.700
Non-Current Assets	**8.400**	**6.400**	**2.400**	**2.400**	**5.400**	**10.400**
Long Term Investments	6.400	4.400	2.400	2.400	5.400	5.400
Other Financial Assests	2.000	2.000	0	0	0	5.000
LIABILITIES	**T1**	**T2**	**T3**	**T4**	**T5**	**T6**
Current Liabilities	**23.300**	**23.300**	**23.300**	**31.000**	**19.000**	**23.200**
Short term borrowings	17.100	17.100	17.100	22.800	10.800	10.800
Other short term liabilities	6.200	6.200	6.200	8.200	8.200	12.400
Non-Current Liabilities	**18.300**	**18.300**	**18.300**	**10.600**	**22.600**	**18.400**
Long term borrowings	14.100	14.100	14.100	6.400	18.400	18.400
Other long term liabilities	4.200	4.200	4.200	4.200	4.200	0
Current Ratio (CR)	**2,00**	**2,09**	**2,26**	**1,70**	**2,61**	**1,92**
General Ratio (GR)	**1,32**	**1,32**	**1,32**	**1,32**	**1,32**	**1,32**

5.3 Graphic disclosure of GR and CR informational content in Internal Events

The Internal Events display an important graphic revelation of the CR's informational content. Plotting the CR *quanta* graph, in the six time periods T, in the Cartesian plane, the informational content shows that there is a non-concave combination because it presents an undefined curve, sometimes concave, sometimes convex, as shown in Figure 9. Thus, in the interval from T1 to T3 and from T4 to T6 the graph presents a concave curvature and between T3 and T5 the curvature is convex. But this curvature depends on the behavior of the CR, if it were constant, only one point or a straight line parallel to the time axis T would be observed. The maximum and minimum points are indicated in T5 and T4, respectively, which are relevant to guide the Economic Agent regarding the decision to obtain the best financial planning.

Regarding the GR, the *quantum* is constant in all time periods, so the curve has zero slope, which is another characteristic of Internal Events. Thus, the GR, in the plane, is a line parallel to the T axis, from T1 to T6.

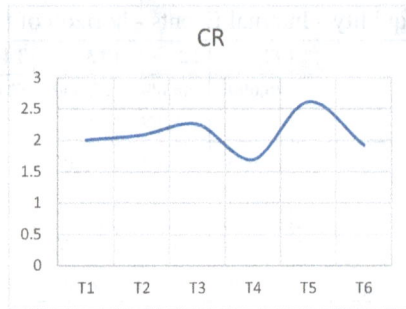

Figure 9: CR curve at times from T1 to T6

6. Conclusions

This chapter contributed to the corporate financial liquidity literature by exposing the characteristics, origin and informational content of the CR and GR ratios, such as nominal payment capacity ratios, which is an introduction to the study of finance.

Nominal payment capacity differs from effective payment capacity or financial solvency because it does not guarantee financial solvency. This occurs because the CR that signals the nominal payment capacity, in the short term, does not match, in a timely manner, the cash inflow dates with the cash outflow dates.

A relevant contribution made by the chapter was the informational content of liquidity, as the main characteristic of the ratios, as well as the concepts of Internal Events and External Events, which signal the origin of liquidity, through the horizontal direction, the cross direction and the vertical direction between the balance sheet aggregates.

7. Quiz 1: Understanding liquidity characteristics test
This Quiz aims to get the reader to understand the main contributions of the chapter. So, answer objectively, marking with "X" the alternative corresponds to the statement, in F or T, being F for the false statement and T for the true statement.

Item	Query	F	T
1	The informational content of the nominal capacity to pay is the main characteristic of the CR		
2	Economic Agent can be a firm, a civil society organization or a government organization		
3	The nominal payment capacity includes concomitant dates of disbursement and disbursement of the Economic Agent's cash flow		
4	*Internal Events* are characterized by the movement or displacement of values between the balance sheet aggregates without any modification of the joint sum of the aggregates involved		
5	*External Events* report the dynamics and continuity of the business, with the inherent risks		
6	*Internal Events* and Outdoor Events are concurrent		
7	By increasing the value of the CA aggregate and keeping the value of the CL aggregate constant, the CR also remains constant		
8	CR curves are defined as convex curves		
9	The balance sheet aggregates, for the purposes of calculating the liquidity ratio, do not admit value adjustment		
10	The informational content of the CR includes the informational content of the QR and the AT		

References

De França, José Antonio and Sandoval, Wilfredo Sosa. (2019). Necessary and Sufficient Conditions for Liquidity Management. International Journal of Economics and Finance; Vol. 11, No. 5

LANCASTER, Carol.; STEVENS, Jerry L.; JENNINGS, Joseph A. (1998). Corporate liquidity and the significance of earnings versus cash flow. The Journal of applied Business Research. v. 14, n. 4.p.27-38.

MYERS, S. C. (1984). The capital structure puzzle. The journal of finance, 39(3), 574-592.

RICHARDS, Verlyn D.; LAUGHLIN, Eugene J. (1980).A cash conversion cycle approach to liquidity analysis. Financial Management. v. 9, r. 1, pp. 32-38.

SHARIFI, Fatemeh and TAGHIPOUR, Elham. (2014). Measuring financial performance using new liquidity indices. Management Science Letters, 4 (2014) 2139–2144.

50

Chapter 3

Analysis of Liquidity Properties

The study in this chapter develops and clarifies relevant aspects of the main properties of corporate liquidity, such as nominal payment capacity, with emphasis on the predictive capacity of net working capital (NWC) to signal the direction of the current ratio (CR), as well as the net long-term capital (NLTC), together with the NWC, to signal the direction of the general ratio (GR).

1. Liquidity properties

The approach of Chapter 2 maintained that the informational content of the nominal payment capacity, measured in the short term, is a relevant characteristic of a liquidity ratio. In this Chapter, the liquidity properties based on the concept and model of Net Working Capital (NWC) and Net Long-Term Capital (NLTC) are introduced, which involve the aggregates Current Assets (CA) and Current Liabilities (CL), Non-Current Assets (NCA) and Non-Current Liabilities (NCL), respectively, from the balance sheet of an Economic Agent.

The NWC model predicts, without any possibility of error, taking the unit as a reference, that the *quantum* of the current ratio (CR) is to the left or right of 1, but it does not quantify the magnitude of that *quantum*, except when CR is equal to 1, because the CCL is equal to zero.

The CCL model predicts, without possibility of error, taking the unit as a reference, that the quantum of the current liquidity index (CLI) is to the left or right of 1, but does not quantify the magnitude of that quantum, except when CR is equal to 1, because the NWC is equal to zero.

The NLTC model does not indicate that it is sufficient to predict the direction of the general ratio (GR) because the GR is a combination of short-term and long-term nominal payment capacities. This combination generates an interdependence of NWC and NLTC in GR pricing. Thus, the chapter's approach proposes and develops a theoretical model of Analysis of Liquidity Properties (ALP) that results from this interdependence to signal the sufficiency of the nominal payment capacity measured by the CR and the GR.

Although current liquidity, recurrent in the literature, is used as a synonym for solvency, in fact, it only represents a nominal payment capacity because operating cycle assets are compared with current obligations, at total nominal values, without normalization of the periods of inflow and outflow of cash, as discussed by De França and Sandoval (2019) who proposed the necessary and sufficient conditions for liquidity management.

From an empirical point of view, even though the existing financial indexes only indicate nominal payment capacity, it seems pacified that they meet the need to assess the liquidity of firms, but, from a theoretical point of view, there seem to be no studies that discuss their properties, and this represents an apparent gap in the literature, including the absence of a relationship with the operational sustainability of the Economic Agent.

In addition to NWC and NLTC, from the point of view of the economic agent's operational sustainability, the Degree of Operating Leverage (DOL) is a relevant predictive indicator of the origin of nominal payment capacity, signaling that the optimal use of installed capacity, that generates assets, occurs when the DOL *quantum* orbits in the vicinity 2, as observed by De França and Lustosa (2011) and De França et al. (2021).

So, the knowledge developed in this chapter can fill the gap identified in the literature, by proposing the ALP theoretical model, by evaluating the characteristics and assumptions of the NWC and the NLTC, individually and together, as indexes of the nominal payment capacity, supported by the logic and linear equation metrics.

The theoretical assumptions of the model are empirically tested, using data from firms from different sectors of the Brazilian economy, whose results are a relevant contribution to the analysis of the liquidity management of Economic Agents in the context of data analysis of financial management.

2. Previous studies

The liquidity and profitability context, as approached by Moir (1997), observes the relationship between profit generation and cash generation, and argues that a firm, in a time interval, according to accounting standards, can generate profits and not generate cash and, in another period of time, it may generate cash and there will be no generation of profits. This contradiction, in the first period of time, may be a consequence of the credit risk that prevents sales from turning into cash; in the second time interval, the consequence may come from the recognition of accounting provisions and non-disbursable expenses that reduce profit, but do not impact cash generation. Thus, as the author addresses, analyzing the consequences of illiquidity is as relevant as analyzing the origin of liquidity, as discussed in Chapter 2. This context clearly indicates that the informational content of liquidity indicators is substantially nominal payment capacity and, therefore, it does not guarantee effective payment capacity or financial solvency.

Based on the empirical finding that the informational content of liquidity indicators is a sign of the nominal payment capacity, especially the CR, the literature has evolved to produce indices with effective payment capacity that signal solvency and financial sustainability of the firm. This evolution occurs through the combination of nominal liquidity with time indicators as discussed by De França and Sandoval (2019) when they introduced the Financial Efficiency Ratio (FER), calculated non-linearly, and the Liquidity Sustainability Ratio (LSR). The authors' contribution shows the combination of non-linear financial efficiency with CR and argues that liquidity is strong when LSR > CR > 1; is weak when LSR < CR > 1 and; finally, the firm's liquidity is insufficient when LSR ≲ CR<1.

The restrictions of the CR's limited nominal payment capacity were signaled by Lancaster, Stevens and Jennings (1998) when they observed the relationship between liquidity, cash flow and financial cycle, but the study by the aforementioned authors did not present an alternative model. An alternative model was presented by Sharifi and Taghipour (2014) who proposed a combination of the traditional variables with the variables of the financial cycle in econometric use with Tobin's model, but the authors' proposition is a linear approach and therefore does not adjust to the nominal payment capacity, to signal financial solvency, as De França and Sandoval (2019), already mentioned, did.

Corroborating the weaknesses of the CR, Richards and Laughlin (1980) also analyzed the contributions of the literature to working capital management. In this analysis, they observed that more attention from managers is necessary for the inefficiency of the aforementioned index, considering that the conventional and static relationships of the financial statements may not be sufficient to guarantee effective payment capacity, because this indicator does not incorporate combinations with the estimators of time.

In addition to the evidence revealed by Richards and Laughlin (1980) and by Lancaster, Stevens and Jennings (1998), De França et al. (2019) researched the relationship between CR and DOL to introduce a model they called Operational Performance versus Financial Solvency (OPSF). The authors state that the model was tested with empirical observations of a sample of 48 firms from 6 sectors of the Brazilian economy, from 2007 to 2017, and that the results obtained provide robust evidence that the firm exhibits sustainable liquidity when it operates at the optimal level of installed capacity, with DOL close to 2, because the CR *quantum* is greater than the DOL *quantum*.

The DOL in the vicinity of 2, as a sign of optimal utilization of the firm's installed capacity, at the level of full employment, was studied and introduced by De França and Lustosa (2011). In this study, the authors understand that it makes no sense to receive DOL lower than 1 because this would mean entropy of the firm's assets and thus there would be no added value. For DOL above 2, the authors argue that there is generation of financial assets, however using partially the installed capacity, and this generation will be smaller and smaller as the *quantum* of the DOL moves away from the proximity of 2.

The study of the relationship between DOL and liquidity was also carried out by Anjum and Malik (2013), however from the perspective of the size of the firm using an econometric model coefficient. The study does not evaluate liquidity properties as predictors of nominal payment capacity and seeks the cause and effect relationship and significance in confidence intervals. These authors conclude that the main determinants of cash holdings are firm size, leverage, net working capital and the financial cycle.

3. Methodological assumptions of liquidity properties

The literature, in a diffuse way, attributes to the CR an informational content of ability to pay. However, this capacity must be understood as being, mainly, nominal because the ratio only reveals a quotient of the division of hybrid aggregates Current Assets (Cash, receivables, inventories and others) by the Current Liabilities of the firm's balance sheet, in a time interval called short term. This time interval measured by the CR, together with the non-compatibility of cash inflow and outflow periods, does not certify it as an indicator of effective payment capacity or financial solvency.

In addition to short-term liquidity, the literature also explores long-term liquidity measured by the GR, as a hybrid indicator because it does not scale a time interval and does not match the terms of cash inflow and outflow periods. Without a temporal dimension, the GR lacks objectivity and therefore does not fulfill the purpose of predicting the ability to honor financial commitments on the maturity date of each debt.

The literature is silent about the informational content of the NLTC as a difference between the NCA and NCL aggregates. Even though the NLTC is not able to predict the GR *quantum*, the migration of values in the NCA → CA direction, and in the NCL → CL direction, and vice versa, is significantly influential in the positioning of the CR.

Once this contextualization is concluded, the basic short- and long-term properties are presented as a basis for the introduction of the methodology of data analysis of liquidity properties. The practical results of the empirical test of the flags, specified by Equations (1) and (2), are shown in Table 2.

$$NWC = CA - CL \gtreqless 0 \qquad (1)$$

$$NLTC = NCA - NCL \gtreqless 0 \qquad (2)$$

The simplicity of these two models may not translate the information content potential they bring to liquidity analysis. The NWC guides the *quantum* sense of the CR. For NWC less than zero (NWC < 0) the CR *quantum* is positioned to the left of 1, that is, CR less than 1 (CR < 1) and the firm will have less working capital. Otherwise, the CR will be, at least, equal to 1 and there it is positioned in the center (equal to 1) or to the right of 1, as described in Chapter 1. On the other hand, from the NLTC it is expected less equity of the firm and more capital of third parties, considering the longevity of the debt that will be paid with resources yet to be generated. These properties will be discussed later in this chapter.

Now, as a simplified way of observing the informational content of the model specified by Equation (1), Table 2 presents the basic properties of the NWC in the pricing of the CR.

Table 2: Basic properties of the NWC

Item	Short-Term Working Capital			Basic properties of liquidity	
				Quantum	Location
	CA	CL	NWC	CR	
1	120	120	0	1,00	Center = 1
2	90	60	30	1,50	Right of 1
3	30	45	-15	0,67	Left of 1

Equation 1 is validated by the three "Item" of Working Capital, in the Short Term, in which the NWC assumes zero in "Item1" and the CR assumes a position in the center with a *quantum* equal to 1, signaling a weak nominal payment capacity. In "Item2" the NWC assumes a value to the right of zero and the CR is positioned to the right of 1, indicating a higher nominal payment capacity. In "Item3" the NWC assumes a value to the left of zero and the CR is positioned to the left of 1, signaling only partial nominal payment capacity, less than 1.

Thus, NWC metrics can be analytically specified as follows:

$$\text{NWC} = \begin{cases} > 0. \text{ It signals CR} > 1. \text{ Strong sufficient or satisfactory capacity} \\ 0. \text{ It signals CR} = 1. \text{ Weak sufficient or satisfactory capacity} \\ < 0. \text{ It signals CR} < 1. \text{ Insufficient or unsatisfactory capacity} \end{cases}$$

From Equations 1 and 2, the methodology that defines the model for the analysis of liquidity properties (ALP) is composed of equations and inequalities that allow observing only the quantitative attribute that shows robustness of the nominal payment capacity, but does not allow identifying any attribute that signals the fragility of liquidity and therefore the qualitative aspect is not observed.

The attribute that exhibits robustness is the CR *quantum* itself, priced only on the basis of financial aggregates, CA and CL, without any combination with time estimators. To signal its fragility or confirm its robustness, as proposed by De França and Sandoval (2019), this attribute requires the combination with ratios of the operational and financial cycles.

The ALP model is divided into two scenarios. The first scenario considers the movement and direction of the CR, based on the premises of the NWC, which reveal the internal generation of liquidity to define the scenario as restricted. The second scenario introduces typologies that combine NWC quantities with NLTC quantities to signal the meaning of the difference between the CR and the GR and define the scenario as comprehensive.

4. Analysis of liquidity properties (ALP)

Liquidity properties are defined in two scenarios: restricted scenario and comprehensive scenario in which the first defines financial planning strategies and the second follows the dynamics of the Economic Agent's business.

The property defined by the restricted scenario, investigates and analyzes the current liquidity model to reveal the generation of liquidity, the movement and direction of the CR as a ratio of the nominal payment capacity.

The property defined by the overarching scenery investigates and analyzes the properties of the overall liquidity to reveal the combination of the NWC and the NLTC and signal the movement and direction of the GR.

For each scenery, the equations/inequalities that make up the model are defined, with their respective metrics, which guarantee their informational content, which is corroborated by the responses of empirical tests, with academic/hypothetical and market data, shown in the following tables.

4.1 Restricted Scenery

Initially, the restricted scenery investigates the internal generation of nominal payment capacity, based on the operational performance design, and then investigates and evaluates the meaning and direction of short-term liquidity defined by the CR, signaled by the NWC, resulting from the difference between the balance sheet aggregates, CA and CL, or even transactions with other aggregates on each side (assets or liabilities) of the balance sheet.

4.1.1 Internal generation of liquidity in the restricted scenery based on operational performance

The operating performance of an Economic Agent is measured by the Degree of Operating Leverage (DOL) defined by Garrison, Noreen & Brewer (2013) as a measure of the sensitivity of earnings in relation to the change in net sales revenue. This performance, as evaluated by Van Horne and Wachowich (1975), occurs because the Economic Agent uses its installed capacity, constant in terms of plant, for a given volume of production, in an estimated period of time, because this implies maintenance and linearity of fixed costs and expenses (FE).

In a study that assesses the optimal level of DOL, controlled by net sales revenue, De França and Lustosa (2011) and De França (2012) present robust evidence, supported by an analytical model, that GAO is a measure of economic efficiency, which signals the optimal performance point when it presents a *quantum* close to 2, whose model was specified and developed as follows:

$$NR_j - VC_j = CM_j$$

$$CM_j = \pi_j + FE_j$$

$$\frac{CM_j}{\pi_j} = \frac{\pi_j}{\pi_j} + \frac{FE_j}{\pi_j}$$

$$DOL_j = 1 + \frac{FE_j}{\pi_j}, \qquad \forall \, \pi > 0 \qquad\qquad (3)$$

In this specification j is the Economic Agent (firm), NR is the net sales revenue, VC is the variable cost (production and marketing), CM is the contribution margin, FE is the fixed costs and expenses and π is the profit.

The graphic representation of Equation (3), plotted by De França and Lustosa (2011), assertively displays the contours of the DOL that signals the full employment of installed capacity in defining the optimal level of performance of the firm. By these contours, the optimal level of performance orbits in the vicinity of 2 is the minimum point of the curve in the first quadrant of the graph. This minimum point is the *quantum* of the DOL in the vicinity of 2. In the third quadrant of the graphical representation, the DOL presents a *quantum* smaller than zero, but this is a paradox as defined by the authors, because negative profit is not satisfactory performance, on the contrary, serves to signal idle fixed costs and expenses.

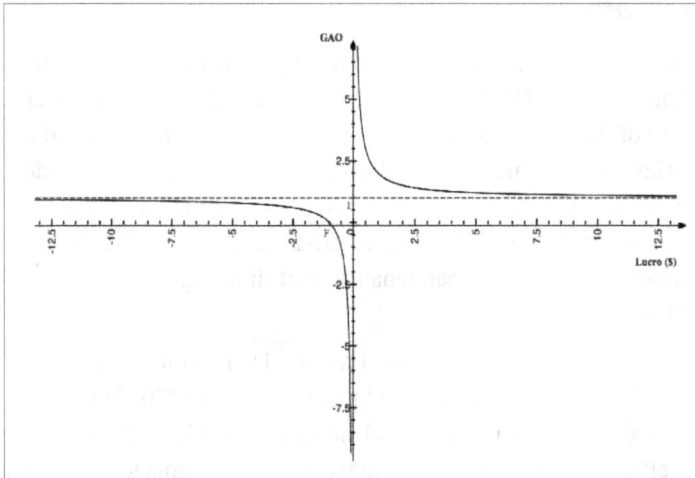

Figure 10: DOL=1+FE/π equation in the plane. GAO is synonymous with DOL. Lucro is synonymous with profit.
Source: From De França and Lustosa (2011)

Further on, De França et al (2021) developed research and presented the binomial Operational Performance versus Financial Solvency (OPFS) to support the relationship between the DOL and the CR in the internal generation of nominal payment capacity, based on the metrics of the OPFS model such as Follow:

$$OPFS_{jkt} = DOL_{jkt} * CR_{jkt}^{-1}$$

$$OPFS_{jkt} = \begin{cases} 1 \text{ se DOL} = \text{CR. Sufficient generation of nominal liquidity} \\ > 1 \text{ se DOL} > \text{CR. Insufficient generation of nominal liquidity} \\ < 1 \text{ se DOL} < \text{CR. Strong generation of nominal liquidity.} \end{cases}$$

In this specification j is the firm, k is the sector of the economy and t is the time.

So, the model's metrics recommend that the lower the OPFS, in relation to the CR, the more efficient the firm is in generating assets with nominal payment capacity.

4.1.2 Movement and direction of the CR based on the position of the NWC in the restricted scenery

In the restricted scenery, the properties of current liquidity are identified by the premises of the NWC greater or less than zero $(NWC^{\pm})$, which meaning the direction of the *quantum* of the CR, to the right or left of 1 or even to the center, when equal to 1. Inequalities/Equation (4) to (6), show how each constrained property is satisfied, in the context of the short-run. For the Economic Agent to be sufficient in nominal payment capacity, the NWC must be positive (NWC^{+}) and the CR must be at least equal to 1.

$$NWC^{+} \Rightarrow CR - 1 > 0 \qquad (4)$$

$$NWC^{-} \Rightarrow CR - 1 < 0 \qquad (5)$$

$$NWC^{0} \Rightarrow CR - 1 = 0 \qquad (6)$$

By Inequation (4) the CR is positioned to the right of 1 (CR > 1) indicating that the firm has a nominal payment capacity to honor its financial commitments in the short term. By Inequation (5), the CR is positioned to the left of 1 (CR < 1) revealing that the firm does not have enough short-term assets to honor short-term commitments. Finally, Equation (6) places the CR at the center (CR =1) and indicates that, at the limit, the firm's obligations can be satisfied with existing assets, in nominal terms, both in the short-term.

But these revelations are not enough to guarantee the CR effective payment capacity or signify the financial solvency of the obligations, as the metrics defended by De França and Sandoval (2019) that combine the financial position with the maturity of the obligations must be observed.

4.2 Comprehensive Scenery

In the comprehensive scenery, the properties of the general liquidity defined by the Interactions of the NWC with the NLTC are analyzed. These properties reveal three scenery of Interactions: (a) Opposite Interactions (OI), **(b)** Unidirectional Interactions (UI) and **(c)** Neutral Interactions (NI).

4.2.1 Opposite Interactions (OI)

The Opposite Interactions scenario is represented by Inequalities (7) and (8) that drive the differences between the CR and the GR, individually, in the opposite direction, according to the combination of the NWC and the NLTC. The direction of the difference shown by Inequality (7), centered on the CR, is to the left of zero, with long-term liquidity showing greater robustness than the short-term. But, in the opposite meaning, the difference resulting from Inequality (8) is to the right of zero, signaling that, in the long-term, general liquidity is less robust than in the short-term.

$$NWC^-, NLTC^+ \Rightarrow CR - GR < 0 \quad (7)$$

$$NWC^+, NLTC^- \Rightarrow CR - GR > 0 \quad (8)$$

4.2.2 Unidirectional Interactions (UI)

Now, we evaluate the Unidirectional Interactions scenery represented by Inequality (9). In this scenery, the quantities NWC and NLTC are either positive or negative ($NWC^\pm$, $NLTC^\pm$), both in the same direction, simultaneously. The differences resulting from this scenery do not present a defined pattern, so the difference may be to the right or left of zero, and it is not possible to define, a priori, which liquidity will be more robust, whether short-term or long-term.

$$NWC^\pm, NLTC^\pm \Rightarrow CR - GR \gtrless 0 \quad (9)$$

4.2.3 Neutral Interactions (NI)

Finally, the evaluation is that of the Neutral Interactions scenario specified by Equation (10). This is not a trivial scenery, but possible, because it predicts current liquidity and general liquidity, both equal to 1, which results in the difference between them equal to zero, signaling balance in the two moments of liquidity, with equivalent robustness.

$$[NWC^0, NLTC^0] \Rightarrow CR - GR = 0 \quad (10)$$

4.3 Analysis of the projection of restricted and comprehensive liquidity scenery

Now in this section, the equation/inequalities models specified in the previous section are used to calculate the *quanta* of the liquidity generation and pricing ratios. Tables 3 to 6 below show empirical test results, with academic/hypothetical and market data, from the narrow and comprehensive liquidity scenery, for the model composed of equations/inequalities from 5 to 10.

4.3.1 Restricted scenery

In the restricted scenery, one of the sources of nominal payment capacity generation is operational leverage and the other is the migration of values between the balance sheet aggregates from the long-term to the short-term, on the asset side, and from the short-term to the long-term, on the liability side, as shown in Chapter 1. This use of short-term and long-term balance sheet aggregates is not restrictive to them, and other aggregates such as FA and NE can be used. The opposite direction of migration signals a drying up of liquidity that reduces the nominal payment capacity.

Operating leverage source

The operational leverage signaled by the DOL *quantum* suggests that an Economic Agent is operationally leveraged if this *quantum* reaches its optimum, as discussed by De França and Lustosa (2011), in the vicinity of 2.

Table 3 presents the results of the combination of the DOL with the CR of 48 firms from 6 sectors of the Brazilian economy (Economic base), from 2007:1 to 2017:4, obtained with the application of the OPFS model specified in 4.1.1. This combination indicates that, on average, firms in each sector operate at full employment of installed capacity because the DOL *quanta* are close to 2, with three sectors to the left of 2 and the other three sectors to the right of 2. The three sectors with DOL to the left of 2 represent 32 firms and the other three sectors with DOL to the right of 2 represent 16 firms.

The informational content of the last column on the right of Table 3 reveals four OPFS *quanta* less than 1, a *quantum* equal to 1 and a quantum greater than 1. The OPFS quanta less than or equal to 1, in five of the six sectors of the economy, confirm that an operationally leveraged firm contributes to the internal generation of nominal payment capacity. However, the sector with a quantum of OPFS greater than 1 also has a DOL close to 2, but the model

61

specification does not capture the adverse effects that may have influenced pricing to the CR.

Thus, in general, considering that a firm's operating assets are generated by sales revenues and that sales are the positive variable in generating profits, at full employment of the firm's installed capacity and, *ceteris paribus*, the DOL varies from inversely to the variation in sales and to the variation in profits, as discussed by Stowe and Ingene (1984) and Gahlon (1981) and, therefore, it also varies inversely to the variation in CR, as shown in the last three columns to the right of the Table 3 (DOL, CR, OPFS).

The results of comparing the CR *quanta* with the DOL *quanta* are a strong signal that the operationally leveraged firm (DOL near 2) generates nominal capacity to pay because for all DOL *quanta* in the lower neighborhood of 2 (less than that 2) the CR *quanta* are greater than the DOL *quanta* and the OPFS *quanta* are less than 1. In the opposite situation, for DOL *quanta* in the upper neighborhood of 2 (greater than 2) the CR *quanta* are smaller than the DOL *quanta* and the OPFS *quanta* are equal to or greater than 1.

Table 3: Internal generation of nominal payment capacity signaled by OPFS - 2007:1 to 2017:448 firms from 6 sectors of the Brazilian economy

Industries	Nr.Firms	DOL	CR	OPFS
IG	7	1,83	2,09	0,88
FO	9	1,68	1,91	0,88
CC	6	2,39	2,38	1,00
H	3	2,72	2,14	1,27
CNC	4	1,80	1,84	0,98
PU	19	1,48	1,91	0,77

Adapted from De França et al. (2021). IG=Industrial Goods; FO=Financial and Others; CC=Cyclic Consumption; H=Health; CNC=Non-Cyclic Consumption; PU=Public Utility.

Internal migration source between short-term and long-term balance sheet aggregates

The migration of values from the NCA to CA and CL to NCL aggregates, from the balance sheet, is the other source of generation of a firm's nominal capacity to pay, as shown in Chapter 1. This restricted scenario, initiated in the analysis of Table 2, is shown now in Table 4 with the variables CA, CL, NWC and CR.

The test of Inequality (4) is validated in *Item2*, where the NWC is equal to 30 and the CR is equal to 1.5, therefore to the right of 1. The test of Inequality (5) is validated in Ord3, where the NWC is equal to (-15) and the CR is equal to 0.667, therefore, the CR is to the left of 1. Finally, the test of Equation (6) identified in *tem1* with NWC centered at zero and CR entered at 1. All these results confirm the theoretical assumptions of the model.

Table 4: Direction of the CR in the restricted liquidity scenery

Item	CA	CL	NWC	CA	Equation
1	120	120	0	1,0	6
2	90	60	30	1,5	4
3	30	45	-15	0,667	5

4.3.2 Comprehensive Scenery

The overarching scenery is shown in Tables 5 and 6, combining the NWC with the NLTC, and identifying the three interactions (OI, UI and NI).

Opposite Interactions (OI). The opposite interactions are represented by the combinations $(NWC^-, NLTC^+)$ and $(NWC^+, NLTC^-)$ shown by Inequalities (7) and (8) above, where the difference between CR and GR is placed to the left of zero (Inequality 7) and to the right of zero (Inequality 8). The academic/hypothetical example, shown in Table 5, reveals the model's assertion (Inequality 7) that for whatever the negative value of the NWC and positive value of the NLTC, at the same point in time, the nominal payment capacity of the Agent Economic in the short-term is less than in the long-term, but the difference between CR and GR may be to the left or right of zero. In *Ord1*, the metric of Inequality (7) is fulfilled, in which NWC is negative (-15) and NLTC is positive (30), resulting in the reduction of the nominal payment capacity of the Economic Agent (CR = 0.667 and GR = 1,2), in the short-term in relation to the long-term, and the difference between the *quanta* of the CR and GR is priced to the left of zero (-0.533). In *Item2*, the metric of Inequality (8) is validated in which positive NWC (30) and negative NLTC (-25) indicate a more robust nominal payment capacity in the short-term (CR = 1.5) than in the long-term (1.037) and the difference between the *quanta* of the ratios is to the right of zero.

Table 5: Impact of Opposite Interactions NWC$^{\pm}$ and NLTC$^{\mp}$ on CR and GR

Item	CA	CL	NWC	CR	NCA	NCL	NLTC	CA+NCA	CL+NCL	GR	CR-GR	Equation/ Inequality
1	30	45	-15	0,667	60	30	30	90	75	1,200	-0,533	6
2	90	60	30	1,500	50	75	-25	140	135	1,037	0,463	7

Unidirectional Interactions (UI). The unidirectional interactions, shown in Table 6, unlike the opposite interactions, are not defined by the sign of the NWC and NLTC. In this construct NWC and NLTC assume the same sign at a specific point in time and the magnitudes of the CR and the GR depend on the magnitudes of the NWC and NLTC, positive or negative. Thus, in *Item1* to *Item4* the direction of NWC and NLTC is to the left of zero and the differences between CR and GR are either positive or negative. Similar behavior appears in *Item5* to *Item7* in which NWC and NLTC are positive and the differences between the two indicators alternate, greater and less than zero, including zero. Then, the results of the empirical test confirm the model metrics of Equation (9).

Table 6: Impact of Unidirectional Interactions NWC$^{\pm}$ and NLTC$^{\mp}$ on CR and GR

Item	CA	CL	NWC	CR	NCA	NCL	NLTC	CA+NLTC	CL+NCL	GR	CR-GR
1	230	480	-250	0,479	190	610	-420	420	1090	0,385	0,094
2	140	151	-11	0,927	390	400	-10	530	551	0,962	- 0,035
3	10	690	-680	0,014	1250	4210	-2960	1260	4900	0,257	-0,243
4	1020	10200	-9180	0,100	250	9350	-9100	1270	19550	0,065	0,035
5	15	12	3	1,250	25	20	5	40	32	1,250	-
6	550	30	520	18,333	20	18	2	570	48	11,875	6,458
7	5100	2300	2800	2,217	3100	952	2148	8200	3252	2,522	- 0,304

Neutral Interactions (NI). In neutral interactions, the impact on nominal payment capacity, in the short and long term, is the same because each indicator, CR and GR, assumes a unit value. This occurs because the NWC and the NLTC, both, are equal to zero, as shown in Table 7, confirming the metrics of Equation (10). Thus, in these interactions there is a balance between the means of payment and the liabilities shown in the aggregates of the Economic Agent's balance sheet.

Table 7: Impact of Neutral Interactions on CR and GR

Item	CA	CL	NWC	CR	NCA	NCL	NLTC	CA+NCA	CL+NCL	GR	CR-GR
1	120	120	0	1	40	40	0	160	160	1	0

5. Conclusions

This chapter revealed a little explored view of liquidity, as a nominal payment capacity, represented by the properties of the short-term and long-term indicators, respectively, CR and GR. It focused on the presentation of recurrent models in the literature and introduced the NLTC construct as a complement to the comprehensive liquidity divided into two scenery: (1) Constrained liquidity scenery to signal the behavior of the CR, to the right and left of 1 and, in the center, when equal to 1, as a behavior reference that represents balance between means of payment and short-term liabilities; **(2)** Comprehensive liquidity scenario composed of opposite, unidirectional and neutral interactions, through combinations of the NWC with the NLTC to jointly indicate the behavior of the two ratios that support the nominal payment capacity. For both scenery, the equations and Inequalities were empirically tested with academic/hypothetical data and market data from the financial statements of 48 firms from 6 sectors of the Brazilian economy, to assess and confirm the power of the model's metrics.

The test with market data showed evidence that the DOL provides robust signaling of the generation of nominal payment capacity when the firm operates at full use of installed capacity, with the DOL *quantum* lower than the CR *quantum* and the DOSF *quantum* lower than the that 1.

The algebraic model developed proved to be robust in terms of liquidity signals such as nominal payment capacity, in the short-term, and in the combinations of NWC with OPFS to signal the meaning of liquidity in the long-term.

6. Quiz 2. Understanding the liquidity properties

Item	Query	F	T
1	The net working capital (NWC) obtained from the aggregates Current assets (CA) and Current liabilities (CL) of the balance sheet signals the direction of the two nominal payment capacity indicators (CR and GR)		
2	Long-term net capital (NLTC) is sufficient to signal that the GR is larger than the CR		
3	The neutral position of the nominal ability to pay in the short-term signals that CA and CL have equivalent values		
4	The restricted liquidity scenery signals the direction of the CR, higher or lower than 1, based on the NWC signal		
5	The comprehensive "one-way interaction" scenery of liquidity indicates that the sign of the difference between the CR and the GR is the same as the NWC and NLTC		
6	In the comprehensive "opposite interactions" scenery of liquidity the sign of the difference between the CR and the GR is always the sign of the NWC		
7	In the "neutral interactions" scenery of liquidity the difference between CR and GR is always zero because the NWC and NLTC are equal		
8	The nominal short-term payment capacity, in equilibrium, signals that the current liquidity ratio is equal to 1.		
9	The comprehensive "neutral interactions" scenery signals that the nominal capacity to pay is in equilibrium		
10	The liquidity property defined by the restricted scenery investigates and analyzes only the current liquidity properties.		

References

Anjum, Sara e Malik, Qaisar Ali. (2013). Determinants of Corporate Liquidity - An Analysis of Cash Holdings. Journal of Business and Management. V. 7, Issue 2, pp 94-100.

De França, José Antonio and Lusbosa, Paulo Roberto Barbosa. (2011). Eficiência e Alavancagem Operacional sob Concorrência Perfeita: uma Discussão com Base nas abordagens Contábil e Econômica. Contabilidade, Gestão e Governança - Brasília · v. 14 n. 3· p. 60–76.

De França, José Antonio. (2012). Eficiência da Firma: Compatibilização das visões da Economia e da Contabilidade. Brasília, 2012. Tese (Doutorado em Ciências Contábeis) - Programa Multi-institucional e Inter-regional de Pós Graduação em Ciências Contábeis UnB/UFPB/UFRN.

De França, José Antonio et al. (2021). Operational Sustainability of the Firm The operational performance versus financial solvency binomial – OPFS. International Journal for Innovation Education and Research. Vol:-9 No-01, 2021. Doi: https://doi.org/10.31686/ijier.vol9.iss1.2909.

De França, José Antonio and Sandoval, Wilfredo Sosa. (2019). Necessary and Sufficient Conditions for Liquidity Management. International Journal of Economics and Finance; Vol. 11, No. 5. Doi: https://doi.org/10.5539/ijef.v11n5p85.

Gahlon, J.M. (1981). Operating Leverage as a Determinant of Systematic Risk. Journal of Business research, 9, 297-308.

Garrison, Ray H.; Noreen, Eric W.; Brewer, Peter C. (2013). Contabilidade Gerencial. 14. ed. São Paulo: Bookman.

Lancaster, Carol.; Stevens, Jerry L.; Jennings, Joseph A. (1998). Corporate liquidity and the significance of earnings versus cash flow. The Journal of applied Business Research. v. 14, n. 4.

Moir, Lance. (1997). Managing liquidity – 2a.ed. Cambridge - England ,Woodhead Publishing.

Richards, Verlyn D.; Laughlin, Eugene J. (1980). A cash conversion cycle approach to liquidity analysis. Financial Management. v. 9, r. 1, pp. 32-38.

Sharifi, Fatemeh e Taghipour Elham. (2014). Measuring financial performance using new liquidity indices. Management Science Letters, 4 (2014) 2139–2144.
Stowe, John D.; Ingene, Charles A. (1984). Microeconomic Influences on Operating Leverage. Journal of Economics and Business, 233-241.

Van Horne, J.C.; Wachowich, J.M. (2008). Fundamentals of Financial Management. 13.ed. London; Prentice Hall, Inc.

Chapter 4

Liquidity sustainability

Liquidity, in the short-term, is a performance measure evaluated by financial rates, centered on the current liquidity ratio (CR), with metrics that indicate nominal payment capacity. But these metrics do not measure financial efficiency or liquidity sustainability, because they do not match cash inflow dates with cash outflow dates, leaving a gap to be resolved in the literature. In order to mitigate the effects of this gap in the study of liquidity, this chapter proposes an analytical combination, in a non-linear way, of the CR *quantum* with the Operating Cycle (OC) and Financial Cycle (CF) *quanta*, to introduce the Financial Efficiency Ratio (FER) and the Liquidity Sustainability Ratio (LSR) which, together, reduce the asymmetry between the nominal payment capacity and financial solvency and, both rates, mitigate the effects of the gap not filled by the CR. The analytical combination, composed of the two rates, is a data analysis modeling that helps the financial and strategic management of an Economic Agent.

1. Necessary and Sufficient Condition (NSC)

Traditionally, liquidity is a performance evaluation measure that uses financial data and indicators, with emphasis on the current liquidity rate (CR), to indicate the nominal payment capacity of an Economic Agent in any of the three economic sectors of the economy (first sector, second sector and third sector), at a given point in a time horizon, resulting from the relationship between current assets (CA) and current liabilities (CL), in a positive working capital environment.

This evaluation measure is incomplete, does not ensure financial efficiency or sustainability of liquidity, because it does not interact with activity ratios, such as OC and FC, to match inflow dates with cash outflows, as argued by RICHARDS and LAUGHLIN (1980), leaving a gap to be filled in the literature.

The discussion about the incompleteness of the CR has motivated studies, in a broad sense, that show the need for a coefficient that has as a requirement the ability to signal, through data analysis, that a firm, belonging to the second sector of the economy, is sustainable in the business continuity.

Being sustainable, in this context, requires the firm to be able to maintain sufficient cash flow to guarantee liquidity; ecologically use natural resources at a rate below the natural reproduction rate; does not produce emissions that accumulate in the environment at a rate beyond the system's natural ability to absorb and assimilate it, does not engage in activity that degrades ecosystem services, and does not fail to produce consistent above-average shareholder returns, as argued by DYLLICK and HOCKERTS (2002); KOELLNER, WEBER, FENCHEL, SCHOLZ (2005); CHRISTOFI, CHRISTOFI, SISAYE (2012). These requirements permeate the Sustainable Development Goals (SDGs) proposed by the United Nations in the Paris Agreement (UN, 2015).

Financial liquidity is the focus of interest and motivation in this chapter, which seeks to fill the gap in the literature, in the absence of interaction between nominal payment capacity and cash inflow and outflow dates, because it combines the activity indicators "operating cycle (OC)" and "Financial Cycle (FC)", when associating with the CR, cash inflow dates and cash out dates, in a positive net working capital (NWC^+) environment.

This gap in the literature is also signaled by the findings of Richards and Laughlin (1980) and, as suggested by Lancaster, Stevens and Jennings (1998), can be mitigated by combining the CR with the activity indicators (OC and FC), which result in the proposition of sustainable liquidity anchored in the financial efficiency of cash flow, as De França and Sandoval (2019) did with the introduction of the theoretical model Financial Efficiency Rate (FER) and Liquidity Sustainability Rate (LSR), as a data analysis tool.

The FER and LSR models were empirically tested with data from 37 firms in the Brazilian manufacturing industry, listed on the B3 (BM&FBOVESPA), in the time horizon 2010 to 2015 (De França and Sandoval, 2019). The results of the tests provided significant evidence that the analytical model makes robust contributions to mitigating the effects of the gap not filled by the CR, because it adjusts the CR, as a coefficient of nominal payment capacity, to signal the effective payment capacity as a proxy for financial solvency of the institution that produce the LSR.

Evidence that signals the Necessary and Sufficient Condition (NSC), such as "Faces of Sustainability and Corporate Liquidity" is anchored in the metrics of Financial Efficiency and Liquidity Sustainability when the LSR *quantum* is at least equal to the CR *quantum* and greater than 1. If a firm meets this condition defended by the LSR sustainability metric, then the firm is financially efficient and sustainable and therefore is a candidate to comply with the SDG proposed by the United Nations (UN, 2015).

2. Literature contributions

This section addresses the main contributions of the literature on sustainability in broad and restricted contexts. In the broad context, studies that address socio-environmental aspects are brought up for discussion. In the restricted context, studies related to aspects of liquidity management are also discussed. Whatever the context of the discussion, interdependence is considered, as one context impacts the other, and the economic result of physical actions that impact social, ecological, financial management and liquidity is disclosed in the financial statements of the entities promoting the actions.

2.1 Broad context of sustainability

Dylllick and Hockerts (2002) argue that an economically sustainable firm continuously maintains a cash flow sufficient to guarantee liquidity, while producing a persistent above-average return to shareholders. They also argue that an ecologically sustainable firm uses the only natural resources that are consumed at a rate below the rate of natural reproduction, or at a rate below the development of substitutes. It does not cause emissions that accumulate in the environment at a rate beyond the system's natural ability to absorb and assimilate it, and it does not engage in activity that degrades ecosystem services.

Koellner, Weber, Fenchel, Scholz (2005), discuss the idea of sustainable investments in the market. They declare that private and institutional investors complement financial information with social and ecological information to assess sustainability, mainly due to the growth of so-called "green funds" that are managed in accordance with the requirements of sustainability and social responsibility. The authors' contribution focuses on the description of the basic principles and methods of sustainability classification, the evaluation of research processes in fund management, as well as the investigation of the fund portfolio in terms of sustainability composition and performance.

Christofi, Christofi and Sisaye (2012) investigated the methods of disclosing sustainable actions and compared the DJSI World, GRI-G3 and "triple-bottom-line" (TBL) sustainability information, using samples of companies from the DJSI World index and from the GRI-G3 list of members, to assess sustainability performance indicators. In their analysis, they found differences in the methods used by DJSI World and GRI-G3 that can lead to inadequate management with systemic, economic and socio-environmental consequences, harmful to citizens and consumers in general.

In a study that explores the role of the business community in promoting sustainable consumption, Michaelis (2003) states that firms assume that their contribution to sustainability lies in improving eco-efficiency, keeping within the range of business behavioral limits. They noted that sustainable consumption requires broader changes that include the incentives that shape the actions of firms and other agents, as well as changes in the culture that underlie market expectations.

2.2 Restricted context sustainability

Richards and Laughlin (1980) analyzed the contributions of the literature to the management of working capital, investments and long-term financing of firms. They observed that working capital management receives less attention than the others, and warn that this inattention to the liquidity management process can lead to inefficiency due to short-term adverse events. Their conclusions suggest that only an examination of conventional and static balance sheet liquidity relationships can bias the firm's liquidity position and to avoid this bias it is necessary to incorporate activity indicators.

Investigating factors that influence the liquidity management of companies in Canada, Gill and Mathur (2011) analyzed a sample of 164 firms listed on the Toronto Stock Exchange, from 2008 to 2010. They argue that the manager has the power to transform assets in his benefit because it has implicit rights to the liquidity of the assets and that a change in liquidity would affect those rights. In their conclusions, they state that firms' liquidity retention is influenced by the liquidity rate, firm size, net working capital, quasi-liquidity, short-term debt, investment, internationalization and business segment.

Lancaster, Stevens and Jennings (1998) analyzed the relationship between liquidity and accrual recognition versus cash flow in static and dynamic aspects. They state that they found evidence that cash flow from operations is significantly related to liquidity ratios and the financial cycle, and that this relationship has an incremental and significant explanation given by revenue for each period.

Lancaster, Stevens and Jenning (1999) empirically evaluated the liquidity of firms in a sample of several segments of different industries based on cash flow conversion variables, extraordinary income, working capital and cash flow from operations. They used static and dynamic measures of liquidity (liquidity rates and financial cycle). They believe that firms within the same industry tend to have the same financial structure, while significant variation in financial structure occurs between industry groupings, but their findings show different impacts of these variables on dynamic and static liquidity for each industry and segment.

Almeida, Campello and Weisbach (2004) modeled liquidity demand to develop a new test of the effect of financial constraints on corporate policies. They establish the constraint conditions and signal that the effect of financial constraints is captured by the firm's propensity to save money from cash flows. They empirically estimated cash flow sensitivity using a sample of manufacturing companies in the period 1971 to 2000 and state that their findings lend robust support to the theory.

3. The traditional liquidity model

The traditional model of short-term liquidity, diffused in the literature, represented by the CR, is specified by the balance sheet aggregates, CA and CL, as shown in Figure 10. This model only signals nominal payment capacity, due to the limitations of its informational content, which does not combine the quantum of the financial indicator CR with the quantum of the temporal indicator of cash flow, FC. For each of the two balance sheet aggregates, there are rules established by accounting that govern the recognition and measurement procedures of transactions allocated to each account that makes up the specific aggregate.

Model	Função
CA	Current Assets, consisting of cash and cash equivalents, receivables and inventories realizable or convertible into currency between two balance sheets or between two consecutive fiscal years.
CL	Current Liabilities, composed of liabilities payable in cash between two balance sheets or between two consecutive fiscal years.
CR	**Quotient of the division of CA by CL (CA/CL) with metrics: CR > 1; CR = 1; CR < 1.**

Figure 11: Specification of the traditional CR model.

The CR financial ratio metrics refer to the nominal ability to pay. They indicate that the nominal payment capacity is satisfactory if the CR *quantum* is at least equal to 1. Otherwise, liquidity is insufficient to honor commitments, considering the period between two balance sheets or between two consecutive fiscal years.

$$\text{CR Metrics} = \begin{cases} > 1 \text{ strong nominal payment capacity.} \\ 1 \text{ weak nominal payment capacity.} \\ < 1 \text{ Insufficient nominal payment capacity.} \end{cases}$$

But even if the nominal payment capacity is satisfactory (strong), it is incomplete because it does not match the signal of cash sufficiency measured by the FC temporal indicator. This incompleteness is mitigated by the model of financial efficiency and sustainable liquidity. See De França and Sandoval (2019).

4. Financial efficiency and sustainable liquidity model

The Financial Efficiency (FER) and Sustainable Liquidity (LSR) model differs from the traditional (CR) model because it combines the *quantum* of the financial indicator (CR) with the *quanta* of the temporal indicators, OC and FC, which indicate whether the compatibility between cash inflows and outflows is sufficient or not so that there is financial efficiency and sustainable liquidity.

It is this combination that suggests that the information content of the CR, transferred to the LSR, is capable of mitigating the gap in the literature left by the CR in signaling the nominal payment capacity of the Economic Agent as effective payment capacity or financial solvency.

4.1 Financial cycle temporal model (FC)

The FC is a combination of the timing of the OC *quantum* with the DPO (Days Payable Outstanding) *quantum* that is the average purchase payment term. Thus, the FC *quantum*, represented by a physical amount of time (days), as shown in Figure 12, is the difference between the OC *quantum* and the DPO *quantum*. So, the FC *quantum*, as it represents a time scale (days), is an assumption that the Economic Agent is financially efficient or not, as indicated by each of its three metrics.

Model	Model specification
P	Period representing the time scale, such as days.
SR	Represents the average balance of sales receivables in period P: $(SR_i + SR_f)/2$ i=initial; f=final
GSR	Represents gross sales revenue in period P (includes indirect tax)
DSO	Days Sales Outstanding: $\textbf{DSO = (P*SR)/GSR}$
SI	Represents the average balance of sales inventories in period P: $(SI_i + SI_f)/2$ i=initial; f=final
CGS	Represents the Cost of Goods Sold in period P
DSI	Represents the Days Sales of Inventory: $\textbf{DSI = (P*SI)/CGS}$
PA	Represents the average balance of purchases payable in period P: $(PA_i + PA_f)/2$ i=initial; f=final
GP	Represents gross purchases in period P (includes recoverable tax)
DPO	Days Payable Outstanding: $\textbf{DPO = (P*PA)/GP}$
OC	Represents the average time, for example days, in which sales receivables and sales inventories are converted into cash. $\textbf{OC = DSO + DSI.}$
FC	It signals sufficiency or insufficiency of cash in terms of time, for example days, in the fulfillment of financial obligations. $\textbf{FC = OC – DPO.}$

Figure 12: Specification of the FC model

The FC *quantum* metrics provide a signal of the Economic Agent's financial efficiency status. Thus, for FC less than or equal to zero (FC ≤ 0) the signal is that, in average terms of time, for example days, the Economic Agent produces enough cash to honor the financial commitments because the cash inflow dates precede the cash out dates. Otherwise, (FC > 0), the cash in dates occur after the cash out dates. It is important to remember that these signals do not mean that there is enough cash, in financial volume, to honor all commitments, but only that the cash inflow occurs before or after the cash outflow.

But it is also known that Economic Agents can obtain cash from other sources to cover immediate shortcomings, such as, for example, raising funds with longer terms and/or contributions from capital owners. These sources temporarily mitigate any cash insufficiency to maintain financial balance.

FC Metrics

$$= \begin{cases} < 0. \text{ Strong financial efficiency because the Economic Agent receives before paying} \\ 0. \textit{Weak financial efficiency because the Economic Agent receives and pays at the same time} \\ > 0. \textit{Financial insufficiency because the Economic Agent pays before to receive} \end{cases}$$

4.2 Financial Efficiency Ratio (FER) Model

The FER model, specified in Figure 13, is an exponential analytical combination that introduces the concept of a firm's financial efficiency. The model specification uses, as variables, the OC and FC *quanta* already specified

75

in Figure 12 previous. It is relevant to observe that the informational content of the *quanta* of the OC and the FC expresses a combination of financial variables with time variables and therefore they are indicators of time or activity as they are disseminated in the literature. Thus, the FER metrics, follow quantified, express the Economic Agent's financial efficiency *status* as a pure number.

Model	Model specification
i	Money cost index (IPCA, Selic, etc.)
OC	Operating Cycle Ratio
FC	Financial Cycle Ratio
FER	**Financial Efficiency Ratio:** $(1 + i)^{fc/oc}$. OC > 0

Figure 13: Specification of the FER model

The FER metrics, follow shown, stratify its information content to signal the *status* of the Economic Agent's financial efficiency. In the first stratification (FER < 1), necessarily, the DPO *quantum* is greater than the OC *quantum*, and the FC *quantum* is less than zero (FC < 0) to signal that the financial efficiency of the firm is strong because the receipt cycle occurs before the payment cycle. The second stratification FER is an identity equal to 1 (FER = 1), occurs if the magnitudes of the *quanta* of the OC and the DPO are equal and, consequently, FC is equal to zero (FC = 0) and the financial efficiency of the firm is weak because the times to receive and pay are simultaneous. Finally, for FER greater than 1 (FER > 1), a necessary condition is that the DPO *quantum* is smaller than the OC *quantum* and, consequently, the FC *quantum* is greater than zero (FC > 0) and the firm is financially insufficient because the cash-out cycle occurs before the cash-in cycle. However, another necessary condition is when the DPO is null, the FER is an identity equal to (1 + i), but by definition the FER is equal to 1 and, in this case, the metric is weak financial efficiency and not financial insufficiency. So, the first metric suggests that the firm is financially efficient and financial efficiency is strong; in the second metric, the signal is that the firm is financially efficient, but financial efficiency is weak; the third metric signals that the firm is not financially efficient, except when the DPO is equal to zero because, in this case, the *status* is weak financial efficiency.

FER

$$= \begin{cases} < 1 \text{ if FC less than zero (DPO} > \text{OC). Strong financial efficiency} \\ \phantom{<} 1 \text{ if FC equals zero (DPO} = \text{OC). Weak financial efficiency} \\ > 1 \text{ if FC greater than zero (DPO} < \text{OC). Financial insufficiency} \end{cases}$$

Now, starting from the FER metrics, its informational content is evaluated, based on the NSC, to present the following theorem.

Theorem

The necessary and sufficient condition for the firm to be financially efficient is:

$$FER \in (0,1]$$

Proof:

[necessary condition]: if the firm is financially efficient, then

$$DPO = 0 \ or \ DPO \geq OC.$$
$$If \ DPO = OC, then \ FER = 1$$

Otherwise, DPO > OC. Logo $\frac{DPO}{OC} > 1 \Rightarrow 1 - \frac{DPO}{OC} < 0$. So, FER $\in$ (0,1].

[sufficient condition]: if FER $\in$ (0,1], then FER $\in$ (0,1).

By definition, FER $= (1+i)^{\frac{FC}{OC}}$. As (1+i) > 1, so $\frac{FC}{OC} < 0$

But $\frac{FC}{OC} = \frac{OC-DPO}{OC} = 1 - \frac{DPO}{OC} < 0$. Therefore $1 < \frac{DPO}{OC}$. Thus, OC < DPO.

Otherwise, FER =1. In this case, by FER definition, $\frac{FC}{OC} = 0$.

If $\frac{FC}{OC} = 0$, then DPO = OC and FC = 0.

So, by definition, the firm is financially efficient and this signals a financial synergy *status*.

Note. For DPO = 0, an economic organization necessarily pays its suppliers in the same period in which it made purchases and, in this context, at the end of the time horizon period there are no purchase obligations to pay. In this case, by definition, the FER is equal to 1 and the firm is financially efficient because there are no obligations to suppliers for purchases to be settled.

4.3 Liquidity Sustainability Ratio (LSR) Model

To assess sustainable liquidity, the liquidity sustainability ratio (LSR) is introduced. LSR is a combination of CR (CA/CL) and FER $[(1+i)^{fc/oc}]$ as shown in Figure 14. The LSR metrics stratify liquidity *status* as strongly sustainable liquidity, liquidity weakly sustainable and unsustainable liquidity.

Model	Model specification
CA	Current Assets, consisting of cash and cash equivalents, receivables and inventories realizable or convertible into currency between two balance sheets or between two consecutive fiscal years,
CL	Current Liabilities, composed of liabilities payable in cash between two balance sheets or between two consecutive fiscal years.
CR	Quotient of the division of CA by CL (CA/CL).
FER	Match interest rate with quotient of the division of the FC by the OC.
LSR	**Combination of CR and FER (CA/CL)/FER = (CA/CL)*(1/FER)**

Figure 14: Specification of the SLR model

The LSR model metrics that stratify the liquidity status, in the definition of strongly sustainable, weakly sustainable and not sustainable, are signaled by the model specification results. So, the first metric defines liquidity as strongly sustainable if, simultaneously, the CR quantum is greater than 1, the LSR quantum is greater than the CR quantum and the FER quantum is less than 1. For the second metric liquidity is weakly sustainable if the CR quantum is greater than 1 and the LSR quantum is less than the CR quantum. Finally, for the third metric, liquidity is unsustainable if the CR quantum is less than 1.

$$LSR = \begin{cases} > CR \implies CR > 1 > FER. \text{ The Liquidity is strongly sustainable} \\ CR \implies CR > 1 = FER. \text{ The liquidity is weakly sustainable} \\ < CR \implies CR < 1 \text{ The iiquidity is unsustainable} \end{cases}$$

5. Informational content of financial efficiency and liquidity sustainability ratios

The empirical test of the financial efficiency and liquidity sustainability model was run using data from the financial statements of 37 firms listed on the B3 (BM&FBOVESPA) of the Brazilian manufacturing industry, which represent the averages of annual periods, of each index, referring to the horizon from 2000 to 2015, shown in Tables 8 and 12 following. Table 8 displays the *quanta* of the current liquidity ratio and the variables that specify the activity ratio. Table 9 shows the *quanta* of the activity index specified by the variables in Table 8 and the *quanta* of the financial efficiency ratio.

5.1 CR informational content

Table 8 shows the *quanta* of the nominal payment capacity index, CR, and the *quanta* of the activity index, DSI, DSO and DPO, referring to the average for the period from 2000 to 2015. Of the 37 firms, 6 firms did not meet the satisfactory metric of nominal capacity to pay, defined by the model (CR ≥1). Firms in this situation are E7, E8, E9, E11, E14 and E19. These 6 firms presented a liquidity *quantum*, lower than 1, insufficient to honor short-term financial commitments, in the horizon between two balance sheets or between two consecutive fiscal years. The remaining 31 firms, 18 exhibit CR with *quantum* between 1.00 and 2.00 and the remaining 13 firms exhibit CR *quantum* between 2.03 and 9.89. Based on these model responses, about 83.78% of the 37 firms present a satisfactory nominal payment capacity *quantum*, between 1.01 and 9.89.

The informational content of the CR's revelations is significant for the understanding that the manufacturing sector of the Brazilian economy presents heterogeneity in its nominal capacity to pay, distributed in firms with strong nominal liquidity, firms with nominal liquidity tending to be weak and firms with insufficient nominal capacity to pay. These data were produced from the model specified in Figure 11 and CR metrics.

The activity index variables were produced from the model specified in Figure 12 and indicate the magnitude of the *quanta* of the OC and FC indexes analyzed in the following section.

Table 8: Ratios of financial liquidity and activity – 37 firms in the manufacturing industry in Brazil – from 2000 to 2015

Firm	CR	DSI	DSO	DPO	Firm	CR	DSI	DSO	DPO
E1	1,01	54,24	45,47	21,72	E20	2,52	71,75	53,28	22,50
E2	3,98	328,12	30,60	35,17	E21	5,33	151,74	47,96	20,68
E3	2,91	56,87	72,35	37,38	E22	1,36	93,46	41,60	27,10
E4	1,89	83,14	155,28	31,15	E23	1,33	53,65	50,46	32,02
E5	2,34	201,76	75,83	30,83	E24	1,89	122,16	90,52	27,81
E6	9,89	84,21	97,09	14,10	E25	2,03	58,93	56,21	19,40
E7	0,78	26,80	46,24	56,19	E26	1,91	274,09	217,08	17,76
E8	0,96	47,83	29,18	84,57	E27	2,45	121,28	68,85	86,72
E9	0,50	67,68	47,05	143,84	E28	3,21	83,47	94,31	26,10
E10	1,09	96,27	77,79	35,84	E29	2,59	123,46	86,97	26,82
E11	0,87	42,72	43,22	44,74	E30	2,50	230,91	132,51	24,30
E12	1,96	93,29	87,86	57,05	E31	1,72	89,08	64,86	33,09
E13	1,75	107,89	49,62	35,64	E32	1,42	368,19	232,46	14,00
E14	0,89	1.233,76	385,82	377,05	E33	1,48	55,48	46,72	19,63
E15	1,82	59,11	27,00	38,86	E34	1,48	108,27	80,94	34,02
E16	3,90	149,95	70,76	23,52	E35	1,90	116,02	42,64	112,68
E17	2,47	55,92	39,29	18,87	E36	1,48	66,73	81,35	83,87
E18	1,54	180,79	35,65	65,30	E37	1,99	40,61	74,54	29,61
E19	0,42	187,97	103,30	162,43					

Source: Prepared from the financial statements of each firm.

5.2 Informational content of OC, FC and FER ratios

Table 9 displays the quanta of the OC, FC FER indexes, run according to the models specified in Figures 12 and 13. The variables used in the specification of the OC and FC models are shown in Table 8 previous.

The informational content of the FC of firms E8 and E9 presupposes "financial efficiency" because the *quantum* of the indexes is less than zero (E8 = -7.5 and E9 = -29.11). The signaling for the other 35 firms E1 to E7 and E10 to E37 is of "financial insufficiency" because the FC *quantum* is greater than zero and, consequently, the FER *quantum* is greater than 1.

These model answers mean that firms E8 and E9 are also financially efficient because they convert sales receivables and sales inventory in a shorter term than the term to pay purchase obligations.

Firms E1 to E7 and E10 to E37 are financially insufficient because the maturity of obligations generated by purchases occurs before sales receivables and sales inventories are converted into cash. So, the metric of the theoretical construct FC smaller than zero, signals financial efficiency by ensuring FER *quantum* smaller than 1 (FER < 1). Therefore, only firms E8 and E9 are candidates for financially efficient *status* because they satisfy this metric. On the other hand, the FER *quanta* of firms E1 to E7 and E10 to E37, as they are greater than 1 (FER > 1), indicate a *status* of financial insufficiency.

The magnitude of the FER *quantum* depends on the magnitude of the interest rate (*i*) and the sign of the model exponent (fc/oc) specified in figure 13. If the sign of the model exponent is negative, the sense (movement) of the FER and exponent of the model, in module, (|fc/oc|), are opposites. This opposite movement indicates that the greater the *quantum* of the model's exponent, in module, the smaller the FER *quantum* when approaching zero (FER << 1). On the other hand, if the sign of the model exponent is positive, the FER and model exponent *quanta* vary in the same sense, indicating that the greater the model exponent *quantum*, the greater the FER quantum.

In addition to manufacturing firms, the informational content revelations of this data analysis are also relevant because financial efficiency is the base of sustainable financial liquidity management.

Table 9: OC FC and FER indexes - 37 manufacturing industry firms in Brazil – from 2000 to 2015

Firm	FC	OC	FER	Firm	FC	OC	FER
E1	78,00	99,71	1,05	E20	102,54	125,03	1,06
E2	323,55	358,72	1,06	E21	179,02	199,70	1,06
E3	91,85	129,23	1,05	E22	107,97	135,06	1,05
E4	207,27	238,42	1,06	E23	72,09	104,11	1,05
E5	246,76	277,59	1,06	E24	184,87	212,68	1,06
E6	167,20	181,30	1,06	E25	95,73	115,13	1,06
E7	16,85	73,04	1,01	E26	473,41	491,17	1,07
E8	- 7,57	77,01	0,99	E27	103,41	190,13	1,04
E9	- 29,11	114,73	0,99	E28	151,68	177,79	1,06
E10	138,22	174,06	1,05	E29	183,62	210,43	1,06
E11	41,21	85,94	1,03	E30	339,12	363,42	1,06
E12	124,10	181,15	1,05	E31	120,85	153,94	1,06
E13	121,87	157,51	1,05	E32	586,65	600,65	1,07
E14	1.242,53	1.619,57	1,05	E33	82,57	102,20	1,05
E15	47,25	86,11	1,04	E34	155,19	189,20	1,05
E16	197,18	220,71	1,06	E35	45,98	158,66	1,03
E17	76,34	95,21	1,05	E36	64,20	148,07	1,03
E18	151,14	216,44	1,05	E37	85,53	115,14	1,05
E19	128,84	291,27	1,03				

Source: Prepared from the financial statements of each firm.

5.3 LSR informational content

Once the CR, FC and FER *quanta* shown in Tables 8 and 9 are known, the next step is the evaluation of the LSR *quanta* by combining the CR *quanta* with the FER *quanta*, as shown in Table 10.

The LSR *quantum* depends on the CR and FER *quanta* according to the model specified in Figure 14. *Ceteris paribus*, if the CR *quantum* grows, the LSR *quantum* also grows. Conversely, if the CR quantum decreases, the LSR *quantum* also decreases. Now, on the other hand, if it is the FER *quantum* that varies, *Ceteris paribus*, if the FER *quantum* decreases, the LSR *quantum* increases and vice versa, that is, in this scenery, the FER and LSR *quanta* vary in opposite sense (movement).

The answers of the model applied to the data of the 37 firms indicate that the 6 firms (E7, E8, E9, E11, E14 and E19) have unsustainable liquidity because the CR and LSR *quanta* are smaller than 1, even though the firms E8 and E9 are financially efficient with strong *status*, with FER *quanta* less than 1. Firm E1 that has a satisfactory nominal payment capacity, with CR greater than 1, also has unsustainable liquidity because the LSR *quantum* is smaller than 1 and less than the CR *quantum*. The remaining 30 firms all have weakly sustainable liquidity with LSR *quanta* greater than 1 (LSR > 1), but lower than the CR *quanta*.

Table 10: Financial efficiency and liquidity sustainability ratios – 37 manufacturing industry firms in Brazil – from 2000 to 2015

Firm	CR	FER	LSR	Firm	CR	FER	LSR
E1	1,01	1,05	0,95	E20	2,52	1,06	2,39
E2	3,98	1,06	3,76	E21	5,33	1,06	5,02
E3	2,91	1,05	2,77	E22	1,36	1,05	1,29
E4	1,89	1,06	1,79	E23	1,33	1,05	1,28
E5	2,34	1,06	2,21	E24	1,89	1,06	1,78
E6	9,89	1,06	9,31	E25	2,03	1,06	1,92
E7	0,78	1,01	0,76	E26	1,91	1,07	1,79
E8	0,96	0,99	0,96	E27	2,45	1,04	2,36
E9	0,50	0,99	0,49	E28	3,21	1,06	3,04
E10	1,09	1,05	1,03	E29	2,59	1,06	2,45
E11	0,87	1,03	0,85	E30	2,50	1,06	2,36
E12	1,96	1,05	1,87	E31	1,72	1,06	1,63
E13	1,75	1,05	1,67	E32	1,42	1,07	1,33
E14	0,89	1,05	0,84	E33	1,48	1,05	1,41
E15	1,82	1,04	1,76	E34	1,48	1,05	1,40
E16	3,90	1,06	3,68	E35	1,90	1,03	1,82
E17	2,47	1,05	2,34	E36	1,48	1,03	1,44
E18	1,54	1,05	1,47	E37	1,99	1,05	1,90
E19	0,42	1,03	0,40				

Source: Prepared from the financial statements of each firm.

5.4 Stratification of the information content *status* of liquidity sustainability

Table 11 shows the sustainability status of liquidity stratified by year and number of observations, in the time horizon from 2000 to 2015, of the 37 firms, totaling 592 observations.

In quantitative terms, there is a predominance of the *status* of weakly sustainable liquidity, with 459 of the 592 observations, which correspond to 77.53% of the total of observations. Strongly sustainable liquidity *status* of just one observation with 0.17%; and finally, an unsustainable liquidity *status* of 132 observations, which corresponds to 22.30%.

This distribution signals in advance that manufacturing firms in Brazil resort to alternative sources of financing to obtain liquidity, either because the financial cycle is greater than zero (FC^+), or because the firms are not financially efficient, or because firms do not meet the nominal liquidity requirement.

These results are consistent with the findings of Gill and Mathur (2011) with regard to liquidity retention and business segment, and in line with the observations of Richards and Laughlin (1980) who suggest that the current liquidity ratio should express combination with activity indexes for an adequate representation of the firm's liquidity.

Table 11: Liquidity sustainability *status* of the 592 observations of the 37 manufacturing firms in Brazil from 2000 to 2015 by number of observations

Year	Not sustainable	Weakly sustainable	Strongly sustainable	No. of firms
2000	8	29		37
2001	8	29		37
2002	10	27		37
2003	10	27		37
2004	9	28		37
2005	8	28	1	37
2006	7	30		37
2007	8	29		37
2008	9	28		37
2009	5	32		37
2010	7	30		37
2011	8	29		37
2012	7	30		37
2013	8	29		37
2014	11	26		37
2015	9	28		37
soma	132	459	1	592

Source: Prepared from the financial statements of each firm.

Concluding the analysis of financial efficiency and sustainability of liquidity, the results provide robust evidence that the financial management of companies in the manufacturing industry in Brazil, in the time horizon between 2000 and 2015, was a sacrifice of finances because, although the nominal payment capacity was satisfactory in 30 of the 37 firms submitted to the analysis, the cash outflows occurred before the respective cash inflows, as shown in Tables 10 and 11.

6. Statistical analysis of financial efficiency and liquidity sustainability

Table 12 shows the estimators of the descriptive statistics of the most relevant variables in the composition of the liquidity *status* that represent the *state of nature* in the research.

The estimators of the variables CR, FC, OC, FER and LSR are demonstrated by the total of observations of the three liquidity *statuses*: strongly sustainable, weakly sustainable and not sustainable.

The relevance estimator for this analysis is the Coefficient of Variation (CV) as it represents the dispersion around the mean. Nevertheless, the analysis of the behavior of the median in relation to the mean (half in relation to the center) is also relevant because it is a support for the analysis of dispersion. Except for the mean of the FER *quantum*, which is placed in the first half of the distribution, the means of all other *quanta* are in the second half of the distribution, with dispersion greater than one standard deviation from the mean. This magnitude of the CV quanta is relevant because it shows that the sectors of the manufacturing industry of the Brazilian economy, on average, grant more time on sales than they get on time on purchases, and this impacts the insufficiency of sustainable liquidity with a recurring need for alternative sources of working capital financing.

The FER *quantum*, as it is the only one that is placed in the first half of the distribution, is the one with the lowest dispersion with CV of the order of 0.022 standard deviations from the mean, approaching the standardized distribution. This information reveals the consistency of the financial insufficiency presented by the set of 37 firms, signaled by the FER metrics, supported by the reduced statistical amplitude between the min and max limits in the 592 observations.

Table 12: Descriptive statistics of the variables of interest from the 592 observations of the sample of 37 manufacturing firms in Brazil from 2000 to 2015

Estimators	Mean	Median	Standard deviation	CV	Min	Max	Obs
CR	2.149	1.676	2.256	1.049	0.079	29.10	592
FC	175.619	119.938	364.469	2.075	-3009.89	5412.44	592
OC	228.926	160.160	341.686	1.492	45.616	5350.33	592
FER	1.046	1.053	0.023	0.022	0.870	1.070	592
LSR	2.0	1.586	2.121	1.039	0.077	27.31	592

Source: Prepared from the financial statements of each firm.

7. Conclusions

Through the analytical modeling of financial efficiency and liquidity sustainability discussed in this chapter, the concept of financial efficiency, the Financial Efficiency Ratio (FER) model and the Liquidity Sustainability Ratio (LSR) model were introduced.

The FER and LSR models were tested using data from the financial statements of 37 companies in the Brazilian manufacturing industry, from 2000 to 2015, by year, by firm and by number of observations.

The results obtained from the data analysis suggest robust consistency of the combination of the *quantum* of the nominal capacity to pay (CR) ratio with the *quantum* of the cash disbursement and pocket (FC) compatibility ratio, to ensure the informational content of financial efficiency and liquidity sustainability assessed by FER and LSR *quanta*.

The research results are promising and can contribute to the literature, academic activities and market professionals, helping managers and researchers to obtain better empirical results. However, it should be noted that the research is restricted to short-term liquidity management and was applied only in the manufacturing segment.

8. Quiz 3: Understanding Financial Efficiency and Liquidity Sustainability

Item	Query	F	T
1	The financial cycle (FC) is a predictor of financial efficiency, it presents a positive *quantum*		
2	The financial efficiency ratio (FER) indicates that a firm is financially efficient if it presents a *quantum* smaller than 1		
3	CR is an ratio of nominal ability to pay		
4	The liquidity sustainability ratio (LSR) indicates that a firm has highly sustainable liquidity even if its *quantum* is less than 1		
5	If the FER *quantum* is greater than 1, the firm has strong financial efficiency		
6	Keeping the CR *quantum* constant, the LSR *quantum* increases if the FER *quantum* decreases		
7	FER *quantum* is greater than 1 if FC has negative *quantum*		
8	If the CR *quantum* is greater than 1 and the FER *quantum* is less than 1, the LSR *quantum* will be greater than the CR *quantum* and greater than 1		
9	The change in the FER *quantum*, *ceteris paribus*, depends on the change in the interest rate		
10	A FER *quantum* greater than 1 signals that the LSR *quantum* will be less than the CR *quantum*		

References

ALMEIDA, Heitor; CAMPELLO, Murillo & WEISBACH, Michael. (2004). The cash flow sensitivity of cash. The Journal of Finance. v. LIX, n. 4 (Aug, 2012).

CHRISTOFI, Andreas.; CHRISTOFI, Petros.; SISAYE,Seleshi. (2012). Corporate sustainability: historical development and reporting practices. Management Research Review. V. 35, n.2, pp.157-172.

De FRANÇA, J.A. & Sandoval, W.S. (2019). Necessary and Sufficient Conditions for Liquidity Management. International Journal of Economics and Finance. V.11, nr. 5.

DYLLICK, Thomas & HOCKERTS, Kai.(2002). Beyond the business case for corporate sustainability. Business Strategy and the Environment. v. 11, n.2, p.130-141, Mar/Apr.

GILL, Amarjit. & MATHUR, Neil. (2011). Factors that influence corporate liquidity holdings in Canada.Journal of applied finance &banking.v. 1, n. 2.Pp. 133-153.

KOELLNER, Thomas.; WEBER, Olaf.; FENCHEL, Marcus. & SCHOLZ, Roland. (2005). Principles for sustainability rating of investment funds.Bus.Strat.Env.nr.14 p. 54-70.

LANCASTER, Carol.; STEVENS, Jerry L. & JENNINGS, Joseph A. (1998). Corporate liquidity and the significance of earnings versus cash flow. The Journal of applied business research. v. 14, n. 4.p.27-38.

LANCASTER, Carol.; STEVENS, Jerry L. & JENNINGS, Joseph A.(1999). Corporate liquidity and the significance or earnings versus cash flow: an examination of industry effects. The Journal of applied business research.v.15, n.3.p.37-46.

MICHAELIS, L. (2003). The role of business in sustainable consumption. Journal of Cleaner Production. v. 11, pp. 915-921.

ONU (2015). In Department of Economic and Social Affairs. Sustainable Development Goals - SDGs. "(https://www.un.org/sustainabledevelopment/blog/2018/07/un-forum-spotlights-cities-where-struggle-for-sustainability-will-be-won-or-lost-2/).

RICHARDS, Verlyn D. & LAUGHLIN, Eugene J. (1980).A cash conversion cycle approach to liquidity analysis. Financial Management. v. 9, r. 1, pp. 32-38.

QUIZ TESTS ANSWERS

QUIZ 1: ANSWERS

Item	Query	F	T
1	The informational content of the nominal capacity to pay is the main characteristic of the CR		X
2	Economic Agent can be a firm, a civil society organization or a government organization		X
3	The nominal payment capacity includes concomitant dates of inflows and outflows of the Economic Agent's cash flow	X	
4	*Internal Events* are characterized by the movement or displacement of values between the balance sheet aggregates without any modification of the joint sum of the aggregates involved		X
5	*External Events* report the dynamics and continuity of the business, with the inherent risks		X
6	*Internal Events* and Outdoor Events are concurrent	X	
7	By increasing the value of the CA aggregate and keeping the value of the CL aggregate constant, the CR also remains constant	X	
8	CR curves are defined as convex curves	X	
9	The balance sheet aggregates, for the purposes of calculating the liquidity ratio, do not admit value adjustment	X	
10	The informational content of the CR includes the informational content of the QR and the AT		X

QUIZ 2: ANSWERS

Item	Query	F	T
1	The net working capital (NWC) obtained from the aggregates Current assets (CA) and Current liabilities (CL) of the balance sheet signals the direction of the two nominal payment capacity ratios (CR and GR)	X	
2	Long-term net capital (NLTC) is sufficient to signal that the GR is larger than the CR	X	
3	The neutral position of the nominal ability to pay in the short-term signals that CA and CL have equivalent values		X
4	The restricted liquidity scenery signals the direction of the CR, higher or lower than 1, based on the NWC signal		X
5	The comprehensive "one-way interaction" scenario of liquidity indicates that the sign of the difference between the CR and the GR is the same as the NWC and NLTC	X	
6	In the comprehensive "opposite interactions" scenario of liquidity the sign of the difference between the CR and the GR is always the sign of the NWC		X
7	In the "neutral interactions" scenery of liquidity the difference between CR and GR is always zero because the NWC and NLTC are equal		X
8	The nominal short-term payment capacity, in equilibrium, signals that the current liquidity ratio is equal to 1.		X
9	The comprehensive "neutral interactions" scenery signals that the nominal capacity to pay is in equilibrium		X
10	The liquidity property defined by the restricted scenery investigates and analyzes only the current liquidity properties.		X

QUIZ 3: ANSWERS

Item	Query	F	T
1	The financial cycle (FC) is a predictor of financial efficiency, it presents a positive *quantum*	X	
2	The financial efficiency ratio (FER) indicates that a firm is financially efficient if it presents a *quantum* smaller than 1		X
3	CR is an ratio of nominal ability to pay		X
4	The liquidity sustainability ratio (LSR) indicates that a firm has highly sustainable liquidity even if its *quantum* is less than 1	X	
5	If the FER *quantum* is greater than 1, the firm has strong financial efficiency	X	
6	Keeping the CR *quantum* constant, the LSR *quantum* increases if the FER *quantum* decreases		X
7	FER *quantum* is greater than 1 if FC has negative *quantum*	X	
8	If the CR *quantum* is greater than 1 and the FER *quantum* is less than 1, the LSR *quantum* will be greater than the CR *quantum* and greater than 1	X	
9	The change in the FER *quantum*, *ceteris paribus*, depends on the change in the interest ratio		X
10	A FER *quantum* greater than 1 signals that the LSR *quantum* will be less than the CR *quantum*		X

CASES AND SOLUTIONS

Case 1

Liquidity characteristics: origins and informational content

1.1 Liquidity as a nominal payment capacity originates from internal events and external events. Internal events generate liquidity from the reallocation of values between balance sheet aggregates, in a vertical direction, without interaction between Economic Agents because the reallocation scenery is the projection of cash without generating new business, as guided by the Pecking Order Theory.

Question. Does the reallocation of an economic transaction between non-current assets (NCA) and current assets (CA), in the CA sense, keeping the current liabilities (CL) constant, increases or reduces the CR *quantum* and why?

Answer. The CR *quantum* increases because the displacement of value is in the CA direction and, as a consequence, there is an increase in the total value of CA and the CL remains unchanged.

1.2 External events generate liquidity in economic transactions with horizontal, cross and vertical direction. These transactions impact the CR *quantum*, increasing or decreasing its magnitude.

Question. Does an economic transaction occurring in a horizontal direction involving CA and CL, in an initial position, impact the CR, increasing or decreasing the *quantum*, and why?

Answer. Yes. An economic transaction occurring in a horizontal direction, in either direction, impacts the CR *quantum*. If the economic transaction reduces the value of CA and CL by the same amount, then the *quantum* of CR increases. Otherwise, if the economic transaction increases the value of CA and CL, by the same intensity, the *quantum* of CR decreases.

1.3 An economic transaction, in a vertical direction, that involves the balance sheet aggregates, current liabilities (CL) and non-current liabilities (NCL) has an impact on the CR *quantum*.

Question. If the economic transaction is in the NCL → CL sense, holding CA constant, what is the impact on the CR *quantum* and why?

Answer. The impact is a reduction in the CR *quantum* because the CL aggregate value increases and the CA aggregate value remains constant.

Case 2

Analysis of Liquidity Properties

2.1 Net Working Capital (NWC) assumes *quantum* to the right and left of zero, including zero. The CR assumes left and right *quantum* of 1, inclusive 1. So, there is a relationship between the NWC *quantum* and the CR *quantum* sense (movement).

Question. What is the condition for the NWC to assume a greater, lesser and equal to zero *quantum* and why?

Answer. The condition for the NWC to assume *quantum* zero is CA equal to CL because CA-CL = 0. For *quantum* to the right of zero, CA is greater than CL because CA – CL > 0. For *quantum* to the left of zero, CA is smaller than CL because CA-CL < 0.

2.2 Degree of Operating Leverage (DOL) is defined as a measure of the sensitivity of earnings to changes in net sales revenue. The optimal performance of the Economic Agent is associated with the full employment of the installed capacity to generate the maximum of financial assets, when the DOL orbits around 2, considering the representation of the model $GAO_j = 1 + \frac{CF_j}{\pi_j}$, where the Economic Agent is identified by the subscript j, the fixed expense is DF and the profit is π.

Question 1. As the sum of the model's income and fixed expenses are equivalent to the contribution margin (CM), in order to generate a greater generation of net financial assets, what should be the behavior of income in relation to fixed expenses, considering constant CC?

Answer 1. MC = Profit + Fixed Expense. It is known that CM = Net Revenue - Variable Cost. So, considering MC constant, if profit increases, fixed expenses decrease. Therefore, the profit must be at least equal to the fixed expense to generate the largest volume of net financial assets.

Question 2. Considering the answer to question 1, is there any profit limit to generate maximum financial assets?

Answer 2. The profit limit to generate the maximum amount of financial assets is associated with the use of full employment of the installed capacity, because beyond this limit, the variable cost can increase marginally and the fixed expense increases in volume.

2.3 The Analysis of Liquidity Properties (ALP) conducted in the research indicates that, the Economic Agent operating at full use of the installed capacity, the DOL is inversely related to the CR.

Question. Is there a logical, technical or intuitive reason for this opposite behavior between DOL and CR *quanta*?

Answer. Yes. At full employment of installed capacity, other things being equal, there is no idleness of fixed costs and expenses and the variable cost of labor is adjusted and proportional to the maximum volume of production, and this maximizes the generation of financial assets or short-term assets. As the DOL orbits around 2 at full employment of installed capacity, the increase in the generation of short-term assets promotes an increase in the CR *quantum*. Thus, for DOL *quantum* much greater than 2, the CR *quantum* tends to be smaller than the DOL *quantum*.

Case 3

Liquidity Sustainability

3.1 The necessary and sufficient condition (CNS) models the LSR *quantum* by combining the CR *quantum* with the FER *quantum*.

Question 1. What is the condition for the FER *quantum* to signal that the Economic Agent is financially efficient?

Answer 1. The condition for the Economic Agent to be financially efficient is for the FER *quantum* to be, at most, equal to 1.

Question 2. What should be the sign of the FC *quantum* to signal that the Economic Agent can be financially efficient?

Answer 2. The condition for the FC *quantum* to signal that the Economic Agent can be financially efficient is that it is, at most, equal to zero.

3.2 The FC *quantum* is impacted by the DPO *quantum*. Based on this premise, the FC *quantum* signals three metrics: greater than zero, less than zero and equal to zero.

Question 1. For FC *quantum* equal to OC *quantum*, what is the condition for the FER *quantum* to be greater than zero less than 1 ($0 < FC < 1$)?

Answer 1. This condition requires the *i* of the FER model to be less than zero.

Question 2. If the FC *quantum* is greater than zero, what does this *quantum* signal to the FER and LSR *quanta*?

Answer 2. For the FER, the signaling is of a *quantum* greater than 1. For the LSR, the signaling is of a *quantum* smaller than the CR *quantum*.

www.ingramcontent.com/pod-product-compliance
Lightning Source LLC
Chambersburg PA
CBHW061837220326
41599CB00027B/5311